THE *Coffee Recipe* BOOK

THE Coffee Recipe BOOK

50 Coffee and Espresso Drinks to Make at Home

DANIEL LANCASTER

Illustrations by Clare Owen

ROCKRIDGE PRESS

First Rockridge Press trade paperback edition December 2019.

Rockridge Press and the Rockridge Press logo are trademarks or registered trademarks of Callisto Media Inc. and/or its affiliates in the United States and other countries and may not be used without written permission.

For general information on our other products and services, please contact our Customer Care Department within the United States at (866) 744-2665, or outside the United States at (510) 253-0500.

Paperback ISBN: 978-1-64152-767-5 | eBook ISBN: 978-1-64152-768-2

Manufactured in the United States of America

Interior and Cover Designer: Joshua Moore
Art Producer: Janice Ackerman
Editor: Kristen Depken
Production Manager: Jose Olivera
Custom Illustration: © 2019 Clare Owen

1 2 3 4 5 6 7 8 9 10

TO MY WIFE, EMILY.
LET'S BE *HONEST*;
I MOSTLY STARTED
DRINKING COFFEE SO I
COULD GO ON COFFEE
DATES WITH YOU.

Contents

Introduction

I F YOU ARE READING THIS BOOK, YOU HAVE PROBABLY encountered "the bean" at some point in your life. I am referring to the brown bean we humans so heavily rely on to get us up in the morning and keep us going throughout the day. Obviously, I'm not talking about a pinto bean; I am talking about the coffee bean.

I first encountered the bean in the form of Folgers being dispensed from a classic coffeepot into my father's "cup of joe" every morning. I avoided it like the plague due to its terrible smell, miserable taste, and the fact that it would supposedly "stunt my growth." Fast-forward to the latter years of high school and my mother's obsession with flavored iced coffees in summer—I started to break down my previous notions. There is something about a lot of cream and sugar that can transform the coffee's bitter taste into something magnificent for a new coffee drinker. Along the way, the high school papers and projects began to add up, and so did my growing interest in the bean. I left high school with an appreciation for coffee; however, this was barely a glimpse of what would be my addiction in years to come.

Freshman year of college I sat in an upperclassman's dorm room while he meticulously groomed his handlebar mustache, all the while measuring his beans down to the gram and pouring water through his gooseneck kettle into a science experiment–style coffee maker. He claimed my mind would be blown–and prohibited my insertion of cream or sugar into the "art" he was making. He was right.

I began gathering my gear as well as tips and tools to perfect my own coffee brewing techniques. This led to an obsession I began sharing online through social media and what then became a website dedicated to making better coffee. Through my journey writing for coffeemadebetter.com, I have explored many facets of the world of coffee and am now fully prepared to share what I have learned with you.

I am here to help you understand the art and beauty of something so simple–a brown bean. I have come to realize that sometimes, the most beautiful things in life can come out of the most ordinary or, in many cases, ugly things of the world. Take dirt, for instance. It is brown, full of decaying matter, and the very thing we trample daily. Yet, when paired with flower seeds, it can produce something absolutely beautiful. Coffee is very much the same. We can either leave it simply as it is–a brown bean–or we can work diligently to find its beauty, present and ready to be discovered within. I have chosen the latter, and I hope I can help you do the same.

This book is meant to prepare you to make exceptional coffee at home. Whether a delicately prepared cup of black coffee or a frozen espresso-based drink for a hot summer day, this book will help you rival any drink typically purchased from your local coffee shop.

There are sections covering the various tools needed to prepare coffee and espresso at home. There are some basic devices you can easily get or may already have, which you will learn to use properly to make amazing coffee at home. You will also learn about more specialized tools that aren't necessary but that can definitely increase your skill set and help you make even better drinks at home. Within the various sections, you'll gain a practical understanding of each device and tool so you can make an informed decision about whether it is necessary for *your* coffee tool arsenal.

But this book isn't just about the tools; it also offers ample advice on techniques for preparing coffee. Making coffee can be as simple as throwing grounds into an automatic drip machine and turning it on. However, there are so many more variables than meets the eye that can alter and enhance your coffee experience. This book will prepare you to make excellent coffee and espresso using whatever method you prefer.

Great coffee and great espresso: check. However, when you add milk and a few other ingredients, the possibilities for amazing craft drinks are endless! Within this book you'll find 50 drink recipes, ranging from classic coffee and espresso drinks, such as Café au Lait (page 44),

Café Latte (page 70), and Cappuccino (page 68), all the way to more specialized drinks, such as a Salted Caramel Frappe (page 124), Pumpkin Spice Latte (page 102), and an Espresso Martini (page 144). These recipes are geared toward the average coffee drinker who may not have all the fancy devices and knowledge but who simply wants to know how to make these drinks in the simplest and most cost-effective manner. While there will be many tools we could recommend, we will teach you the basics of making these drinks, as well.

Wherever you are in your journey through the world of coffee, this book is meant to meet you where you stand and help you proceed forward. Coffee is truly a delight. It is my hope this book helps you fall even more deeply in love with "the bean" than you already are.

CHAPTER ONE

The Basics

MAKING COFFEE AT HOME CAN BE INCREDIBLY REWARDING.
Being able to kick back on your couch, bed, or porch with a nice
book and a cup of coffee is something you would be hard-pressed
to complain about. However, many people opt to spend hundreds
of dollars a year buying coffee at coffee shops and cafés instead
of having the satisfaction of making it themselves at home. The
root of the problem is that many people assume they will not be able
to make the same quality coffee at home as what they can buy at the
nearest coffee shop. I'm here to tell you this assumption is not true!

This chapter will teach you how to make amazing coffee at
home—without elaborate or expensive equipment. You don't need to
spend hundreds of dollars on upgrading your gear, and you don't even
need to grow a fancy mustache or wear a hipster fedora like your local
baristas (unless you really want to!). With items you probably already
own, you can successfully recreate most any of your favorite coffee

and espresso drinks. To get you started on your at-home coffee journey, this chapter provides an overview of the basic tools and devices needed to make great coffee and espresso at home. Not only will you learn about equipment, but you'll also pick up some great tips and techniques so you have everything necessary to make your own coffee drinks that will rival any from your local coffee shop.

THE BEANS

The duration of time coffee beans are roasted is a critical step in determining how a cup of coffee will taste. It may surprise you to learn that before being roasted, coffee beans are actually a soft bean with a greenish-yellow color. It is the process of roasting the beans that transforms these flavorless beans into either a sweet, fruity, acidic cup of coffee or a dark, bitter, strong cup of coffee—depending on how long they are roasted.

LIGHT ROAST

During the roasting process, the coffee beans crack once they reach an internal temperature of about 400°F. Generally speaking, light-roast coffee beans are those that have not yet reached their "first crack." Because the beans are not roasted for very long, a cup

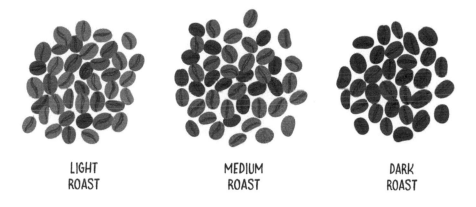

LIGHT
ROAST

MEDIUM
ROAST

DARK
ROAST

of coffee made from a light roast would have more fruity, floral, and acidic flavor notes. Light-roast coffees are often referred to in stores as "Half City Roast" or "New England Roast."

MEDIUM ROAST

Medium-roast coffees are generally those that have been roasted between the first crack, at an internal temperature of about 400°F, to before the second crack, or an internal temperature of 428°F. A cup of coffee made from a medium-roast would exhibit a smoother, more balanced flavor with a mildly intensified degree of bitterness when compared to a light-roast coffee. Medium-roast coffees can often be referred to as "City Roast" or "Breakfast Roast."

DARK ROAST

Dark-roast coffees are roasted past the second crack, to an internal temperature of roughly 464°F, which is about as far as you can go without ruining a coffee bean. One quality worth noting is that dark-roast beans have an oily shine to them as a result of the roasting process, which pulls oils from inside the coffee bean to the outside. A cup of coffee made from a dark roast would exhibit smoky, bitter, and burnt flavors. Dark-roast coffees are often referred to in stores as "French Roast" or "Italian Roast."

FUN FACT: We're hooked! Did you know Americans consume 400 million cups of coffee per day? That's equivalent to 146 billion cups of coffee per year! Considering there are only roughly 329 million people in the United States, we may have a bit of an obsession.

THE GRINDERS

One critical decision in the coffee brewing process is whether to buy whole beans to grind yourself or pre-ground coffee. For optimal freshness, whole beans are the better choice because when the cells inside the coffee beans are exposed to air, the volatile aromas react and oxidize. This oxidation results in a 60 percent loss of aroma and flavor within 15 minutes of being ground. If you prefer pre-ground coffee, that is fine, but should you want to try whole-bean coffee, here is a little information on grinders.

BURR GRINDERS

Burr grinders are made of two disks called burrs that funnel the beans through the grinder. One of the burrs is stationary while the other rotates to break up the beans. This grinding method results in more uniformly sized coffee grounds. Typically, burr grinders also allow you to adjust how far apart the burrs are so you can choose to grind your beans as coarsely or as fine as you like. One thing to note about burr grinders is that they are typically more expensive than blade grinders, at around $30 on the low end.

BLADE GRINDERS

Blade grinders grind the beans by using a single propeller-style blade that spins. These grinders typically grind beans faster and are a little bit cheaper than burr grinders, at around $10 on the low end. The one drawback is they do not always produce a very even grind, resulting in some grounds being very coarse while others are very fine. Different-size grounds are a problem because when brewed, they will produce strange flavors in your coffee. The finer grounds will lose their flavor more quickly than the coarse grounds while being brewed and pro-duce a bitter taste.

GRINDING GUIDE

Depending on which brewing device you use to make coffee, there are different optimal levels of how coarsely or finely ground the coffee should be. Here is a simple chart to help you when brewing coffee by various methods.

LEVEL OF GRIND	COFFEE BREWING DEVICE
EXTRA FINE	Cezve coffee maker (Turkish Pot)
FINE	Moka pot/stovetop espresso, espresso machine, AeroPress (fine-medium depending on preference), coffee cupping
FINE-MEDIUM	V60 Pour Over, Kalita Wave Pour Over, Bonavita coffee dripper
MEDIUM	Siphon/vacuum pot, drip machines
MEDIUM-COARSE	Chemex, Clever Dripper
COARSE	French press, percolator
EXTRA COARSE	Cold brew, cowboy coffee

THE FILTERS

Filters are an essential ingredient when making coffee, as they allow the wonderful flavors you want in your cup to pass through but leave behind the excess grounds you would rather keep out of your coffee cup. There are different kinds of filters that, in turn, allow more or fewer coffee particles to pass through into your beverage, and each has its own advantages and disadvantages.

PAPER

Paper filters are the most popular choice for pour-over methods, as they are affordable and allow the least amount of coffee oils and particles to pass through, which results in a clean and vibrant cup of coffee. Specialty coffee enthusiasts love the paper filter for its ability to highlight the best flavors in coffee while leaving the excess behind. One downfall is that paper filters can leave an earthy, papery taste in your coffee. One way to help minimize this is to rinse your filter before you brew your coffee. Due to the single-use nature of paper filters, some people prefer to use cloth and metal filters to reduce their environmental footprint.

CLOTH

Cloth filters are not very common except for use in siphon coffeepots. Cloth filters are made of various types of fabric that are thin enough to allow water to pass through. These are great if they are clean, as they do not allow for as much "sludge" to pass through the filter into the drink. However, after many uses, cloth filters will often transfer a wet sock flavor into your cup of coffee, which, for obvious reasons, is undesirable.

METAL

Metal filters are used most commonly for the French press and pour-over methods of coffee making. The metal filter allows larger coffee particles to pass through it compared to paper and cloth filters. This can often result in "sludge" at the bottom of a cup of coffee made with a metal filter. This sludge is composed of different oils and fine coffee particles that can result in a creamier, stronger coffee taste that, to some, is desirable and to others is off-putting.

Coffee Break! BRIEF TIMELINE AND HISTORY OF COFFEE

850 CE: The coffee bean is discovered by an Ethiopian herdsman who observed his goats acting in a strange manner after eating red berries from a coffee bush. Legend says that the herdsman showed the beans to local monks, who thought they were from the devil and, in turn, threw them into a fire. This resulted in the  pleasant aroma of fresh-roasted coffee, which then prompted them to find a way to consume it. Somewhere along the way, they figured out they could chop it up and mix it with water to make a delicious and energizing beverage!

1000: The first known piece of literature describing coffee by philosopher Avicenna Bukhara is recorded.

1454: The first coffee houses, which double as spaces for religious practices, are established in Ethiopia, called Kaveh Kanes.

1511: In Mecca, citizens gather in coffee houses to discuss political issues. The governor, fearful of the influence these gatherings produce, bans coffee and has the coffee houses shut down.

1570: Coffee arrives in Venice, which then facilitates the spread of coffee across the world.

1800s: Global coffee consumption skyrockets with the growth of companies such as Folgers and Maxwell House.

1884: Angelo Moriondo receives the patent for the first espresso machine.

1908: Melitta Bentz patents the coffee filter.

1971: Starbucks opens its first store in Seattle and helps initiate the "second wave" of coffee, focused on increasing the quality of coffee.

1982: The Specialty Coffee Association is formed to help foster and support innovation within the high-quality coffee market.

2002: The term "third wave" is coined by Trish Rothgeb of Wrecking Ball Roasters, who compares specialty coffee workers to artisans due to the level of care they devote to the product throughout the entire coffee-making process—from crop to cup.

PRESENT DAY: We see a growing interest in specialty coffee and practices to help shape the trajectory of coffee in the future!

THE DEVICES

There are a variety of devices that can be used to make great coffee or espresso at home. Some are very simple to use, while others have more intricate features. This section provides an overview of some of the more popular devices and what they are best used for.

AUTOMATIC DRIP BREWER

The automatic drip brewer is the standard across America for making a quick, classic cup of coffee. Most homes are equipped with one of these, and they seldom sit unused. The first automatic drip brewer by Mr. Coffee hit the market in 1972. By 1974, half of the 10 million coffee makers sold in America were automatic drip brewers. The legacy of this brewer lives on today as a classic way to make coffee, steeped in family tradition. There is nothing like the sweet sound of a drip machine bubbling as the coffee slowly drips into the carafe, where enough coffee for the entire family can be made. This method is certainly the easiest option for someone on the go, as all you need to do is put the grounds and water in the machine and click START! After five minutes or so, you have an entire pot of coffee! Another plus: This device is sold almost everywhere, ranging in price from $10 to $300, depending on the features you are looking for. If you are open to a used machine, you can bet on finding multiple choices at any thrift store or yard sale for $1 or $2.

PERFECT FOR

The automatic drip brewer is the best way to brew coffee for a large group. Most machines can make at least 10 to 12 cups at a time (some even more), and it takes only a few minutes. The machines are also very hands-off, which allows you to start the coffee and walk away until it is finished. The only downfall to them is that these machines are not known for producing exceptional coffee unless you are willing to spend hundreds of dollars to buy one that imitates a manual pour over. The lower-end models simply dump water on the grounds at an uncontrolled speed and temperature, which often causes the coffee to be burned and underextracted, resulting in a less-than-perfect taste.

MANUAL POUR OVER

You would be remiss if you attempted to get into specialty coffee and knew nothing about the manual pour over. This method has been around since its invention in 1908; however, in recent years it has become the most popular specialty coffee brewing method in shops and homes worldwide. The pour over is precisely what the name suggests: You pour hot water over coffee grounds held within a filter basket or cone-shaped paper filter. The most popular pour-over devices are the Chemex and the Hario V60 dripper.

The Chemex was invented by Dr. Peter Schlumbohm, a chemist (hence the name). It quickly grew in popularity due to its visually strik-ing design and the way it was able to brew coffee using nonporous glass without imparting any flavors of its own into the cup.

The Hario V60 is very similar in design but can sit atop your mug for easy use and portability. The average cost of a manual pour over ranges from $10 on the low end for plastic models and up to $40 on the high end for the glass Chemex coffeepot.

The reason the pour-over method has become so popular among coffee enthusiasts is due to the degree of control it gives the barista. It allows you to pour water at a controlled rate and pattern for optimal extraction from within the coffee grounds, giving you a much better cup of coffee.

PERFECT FOR

Pour overs are perfect if you have higher-quality coffee with vibrant flavor notes. The pour over has the unique and unrivaled ability to really pull out the sweet and delicate flavors in the coffee beans. The downside is that the process can be a bit tricky to master and first attempts can result in some inconsistently strange cups of coffee. However, once you get the hang of it, the pour over can produce a well-rounded, gentle, clear cup of coffee. Another thing to note with this method is that it is typically not ideal for making coffee in large quantities. There are higher-volume versions of the Chemex, but most pour overs are geared for 1 to 2 cups at a time and often take a few minutes of your undivided attention for best results. That said, if you are willing to give it the time and effort, it is well worth it!

FRENCH PRESS

Aside from the automatic drip brewer, the French press is one of the most popular home brewing methods around, and for good reason. Brewing a decent cup of morning coffee on a French press is nearly guaranteed, making it accessible to even the most amateur coffee brewers. The brewing process consists of pouring hot water over the grounds, letting them brew for 3 to 4 minutes, and pressing the metal filter down, pushing the coffee grounds to the bottom of the pitcher. This immersion method of brewing is often attributed to a Frenchman from the 1800s who forgot to add his coffee to the pot before boiling the water. After adding the grounds to the already boiling water, he noticed they all floated at the top. Not wanting to waste the precious beverage, the man used a metal screen and a stick to push all the grounds to the bottom of the pot, resulting in a nicely brewed cup of coffee.

Today, the French press is popular for its ease of use and versatility. In addition to brewing hot coffee, this device can be used to make cold brew, tea, and even frothed milk! One negative aspect of using the French press is that there is often a noticeable amount of "sludge" at the bottom of your cup due to the larger holes in the metal filter.

However, some people enjoy the thickness that comes from coffee sediment. It's a personal preference. The French press is very easy to find in stores or online and can be purchased for $20 to $30.

PERFECT FOR

The French press is a great option for those who enjoy a richer, medium-bodied cup of coffee but still need something simple and user-friendly. The French press is easy to use and is something you can start and walk away from for a few minutes, rather than having to meticulously tend the coffee. The French press is an immersion method that often produces more robust, creamy flavors rather than the fruity, vibrant flavors of the pour-over method. The taste can, in many ways, be likened to the rich comfort of a cozy blanket by the fireplace on a snowy winter's eve.

AEROPRESS

The AeroPress did not hit the market until 2005, making it the newbie of coffee brewing devices. It was developed by an engineer who spent years researching ways to create the best single-serve brewing device. The result is an incredibly smooth cup of coffee made in a fraction of the time other methods can take and with very little hassle. Its most common use is for making espresso-like coffee. The AeroPress is technically an immersion method of brewing, but the short brewing time comes from the use of a smaller grind size. A plunger is inserted into the device, and trapped air pushes the water through a small paper filter and directly into your cup. The AeroPress is low maintenance, portable, and easy to use. It's a great option to bring along when you travel, as it is small and made of plastic. These brewers can be found online and in many stores and cost about $30. One drawback is that the AeroPress is not a great option for making coffee for all your friends, as it is, by nature, a single-serve brewing device.

The AeroPress has been praised repeatedly for its ability to make espresso-like coffee in such a short amount of time and without all the expensive gear that comes with making espresso. The AeroPress has gained such momentum that in recent years there is actually a World AeroPress Championship each year, where participants compete to make the best espresso using this device.

MOKA POT

The Moka pot was invented by Luigi di Ponti and Alfonso Bialetti in Italy in 1933 and has been a classic ever since. The Moka pot is a stovetop coffee maker that brews coffee by passing water that is pressurized by steam through a bed of grounds placed above it. The idea behind the Moka pot was to make espresso at home without the expensive equipment. At the time, it was certainly the best and most affordable alternative! Today, you find many different versions of the Moka pot; however, the most popular is the Bialetti, which is made of aluminum and has eight sides for even heat distribution. Although it is no longer at its peak of popularity compared to other brewing methods, it has had a resurgence lately within the specialty coffee community. Its affordability, at roughly $25, and the aesthetic of a tiny pot of espresso gurgling on the kitchen stove are what draw people back to the timeless classic.

PERFECT FOR

The Moka pot rivals the AeroPress as the easiest, most affordable home method of brewing espresso. It produces a full-bodied, sweet, and, often called, "viscous" shot of espresso. It is an amazing option if you do not have the money to buy a full-out espresso machine. Another convenient attribute of the Moka pot is its small size. It is extremely portable and also makes any kitchen look supremely "cute" simply by its presence.

ESPRESSO MAKER

The espresso machine originated in Italy in the early 1900s. It was brought to the United States in the 1920s and can be found in virtually any coffee shop today. For our purposes, however, we will focus on home espresso makers rather than the large commercial machines found in most coffee shops. Having access to an at-home espresso machine has only been a reality for about the last 20 years. As you might guess, the price point for these machines is on the higher end, averaging several hundred dollars for a good machine. The espresso maker is good for just that: making espresso.

Espresso is made when hot water is quickly forced through very finely ground coffee. It is typically made in "shots" of 1 to 2 ounces. The upside of having a home espresso maker includes being able to quickly create a variety of espresso drinks that may take more time without an actual machine. In addition, most espresso makers have the ability to steam and froth milk, and many can even grind beans. However, keep in mind that most home espresso makers simply cannot make the same quality espresso as a much more expensive commercial machine, so many people argue it is not worth the money. They also require regular maintenance to keep them in good working condition.

PERFECT FOR

These expensive machines are perfect for those who truly love espresso as their daily drink of choice. This can be in the form of a plain shot of espresso or as a latte, frappe, or cappuccino. Most people who own an espresso machine use it to make specialty drinks that require espresso. The other beauty of the espresso machine is that it is great for hosting a crowd, as you will be able to make amazing drinks that stand apart from a simple cup of coffee.

THE MILK

Many coffee beverages require either steamed or frothed milk. Steamed milk is essentially milk that has been heated. Steaming milk brings out its natural sweetness and creates a slightly thicker texture. Steamed milk is responsible for the creaminess of a latte, among other drinks. Frothed milk has more air whipped into it and, therefore, less liquid, and adds a thick layer of foam on top of many drinks, such as a cappuccino.

MILK FROTHER

A milk frother is a relatively inexpensive device used to create frothed milk. A small handheld milk frother can be purchased for $10 to $15 and quickly and easily creates that foamy goodness you need to top off your homemade cappuccino.

MILK STEAMER

A milk steamer is often found on more expensive home espresso makers and requires an additional steaming pitcher for use. Steamers are convenient because they inject air into the milk at high speeds, thereby creating froth, while simultaneously heating the milk. This saves time and prevents the milk from cooling during the frothing process. However, these machines are much more expensive and therefore less accessible to the average person.

MILK ALTERNATIVES

Although whole milk gives the best results when steaming or frothing milk, it is not the only option. Soymilk is a good alternative for getting a creamy texture and thick foam without the dairy. Almond milk offers a sweet, nutty flavor but doesn't thicken up very well when frothed. A newer popular milk alternative in the coffee world is oat milk, which has a milder flavor than almond milk and froths and steams well.

CHAPTER TWO

Your Best Brew

THERE ARE MANY FACTORS INVOLVED IN BREWING A GREAT cup of coffee. One of the most important is the devices we have already explored. However, the final result comes down to so much more than just having the right gear. You could have the best grinder, the best pour over, and the best gadgets, but without proper technique, you could still produce terrible coffee. This chapter gives you the five most important rules to consider when brewing coffee. These rules translate to all devices and give you a well-rounded approach to produce amazing results when you brew coffee at home.

And though there are certainly hundreds of tips and techniques I could offer, these are the five that will set you apart and be most beneficial no matter what coffee brewing skill level, knowledge, or gear you have.

Now, I want to make it clear that if you don't follow all of these rules all of the time, it doesn't mean your coffee will not be good.

I have made coffee without following all these steps, and it has still turned out awesome. These steps are simply guideposts for you and, when followed, will increase the potential for some amazing coffee.

Rule 1: PICK THE RIGHT BEANS

This is by far the most important rule of all. The entire goal of this book is to help you pull out the best possible flavors from the bean, and if the flavors within the bean aren't good . . . we have a problem. Start with the highest-quality coffee possible depending on your location and budget. Here are a few pointers when it comes to picking the right beans.

ROAST DATE: Buy beans that have been roasted as recently as possible. The more recently they were roasted, the better they will taste. You can have the most expensive coffee in the world, but if it has been a few months since it was roasted, it really doesn't matter how nice it was in the first place.

BUY ARABICA: This is huge. Make sure the beans are of the "arabica" varietal, rather than "robusta," as they are much higher quality and have a sweeter, more balanced flavor. Robusta beans tend to be very bitter and not very exciting.

ORGANIC VERSUS NONORGANIC: This is by preference. Organic coffee, obviously, has not been exposed to as many chemicals and, typically, has been produced under better standards for the workers who come into contact with it. The only downside is that some coffee professionals have found that some higher-quality coffees do not survive well unless at least a small degree of pesticides are used during their growth. This results in some of the best coffee around the world not being certified as organic.

GROWING LOCATION: Coffee beans are grown all over the world. The amazing thing is that a coffee bean grown in Brazil will taste very different from a coffee bean grown in Ethiopia. The climate, soil, elevation, and many other regional variables all affect the coffee beans' flavor. The next page shows a basic chart to help you recognize characteristics from different coffee-growing regions.

This chart is a general aid for understanding what coffees from different regions will taste like, but there are so many variables that can completely change the taste of coffee. The best way to fully understand what you like is to try as many different kinds as you can!

GROWING AREA	FLAVOR CHARACTERISTICS
BRAZIL	Bittersweet chocolate, heavy-bodied
BURUNDI	Chocolate, floral, vanilla
COLOMBIA	Balanced, medium-bodied, nutty, sweet
COSTA RICA	Bright, citrusy, nutty, sweet
ETHIOPIA	Berry, floral, fruity, lemon
GUATEMALA	Floral, honey, smoky, spicy, sweet
INDONESIA	Bitter, earthy, heavy-bodied, low acid, spicy
JAVA	Bitter, earthy, heavy-bodied, woody
KENYA	Black currant, floral, fruity, grapefruit, juicy, spices
MEXICO	Balanced fruit and spice, light-bodied
PERU	Acidic, rich caramel, soft, sweet
SUMATRA	Bitter, earthy, smoky, syrupy

Rule 2: GRIND IT YOURSELF

The goal of coffee farmers, roasters, and baristas is to coax the most flavor possible out of a coffee bean. Grinding the beans ahead of time discounts much of the work that has gone into producing the coffee. When the cells inside the coffee beans are exposed to air, they begin reacting to it and lose aroma and flavor every second after. A day or two after being ground, the coffee will have lost almost all its flavor. If your coffee has been ground for 5 or 6 days, it has essentially lost all its flavor, and it is almost irrelevant how much longer you keep it—it is a lost cause.

The oils in the coffee also begin to dilute from exposure to the moisture in the environment when coffee beans are ground. These coffee oils are delicate and are easily contaminated. Whatever other odors or aromas are near your grounds can form inside your beverage.

It's also worth noting that carbon dioxide plays a major role in getting the essential oils into the coffee after they're released. The problem is that ground beans now have an increased surface area that is exposed (compared to whole beans, which simply expose the outer shell) to air and other contaminants. When grounds are exposed, the carbon dioxide is released. Within 60 seconds of grinding coffee beans, 80 percent of the gas is released into the air (that's why it smells so good). It then begins to multiply in loss in the minutes following. This reaction results in exponential flavor loss. For the most flavor, simply wait until the last minute before brewing to grind your beans.

Rule 3: WATER TEMPERATURE

For the perfect cup of coffee, one of the most important yet most neglected steps is brewing coffee at the right water temperature. If your water is too hot, you risk overextraction of coffee flavors and, in turn, a burnt, bitter cup. If your water is too cold, you risk under-extraction of coffee flavors and, in turn, a weak, sour cup. The goal is to find yourself right in the middle of those two temperatures, at which you will be able to extract the most flavor from a bean without imparting any unwanted tastes.

According to the National Coffee Association, the perfect temperature to brew a cup of coffee is between 195°F and 205°F. That leaves a gap of 10 degrees, so depending on your preference (whether you like it more bitter or not), you can choose the exact temperature at which you want to brew. Any temperature outside this range risks overextraction or underextraction.

You may be asking why 195°F to 205°F? This temperature range is where water-soluble flavor compounds dissolve in water easiest.

If you don't have a thermometer, you can still monitor your water temperature. If you live at sea level, simply bring the water to a boil and wait a minute or two before brewing. However, if you live at a high elevation, brew the coffee immediately after the water boils. At 5,000 feet of elevation, water boils at 202°F, which would be right within the range to brew the best coffee. If you live 7,000-plus feet in elevation, let the water rise in temperature a little bit after it boils before you brew the coffee.

BONUS TIP: Aim on the lower temperature side for darker roasts and on the higher side of temperature for lighter roasts!

Rule 4: WEIGH IT

The amount of coffee grounds you use in relation to the amount of water you use is a critical variable to nail down when brewing coffee. When water extracts flavor from coffee grounds, the first flavor that comes from the grounds is sour, then comes the classic rich coffee flavor, and after the rich flavor is extracted, then comes the bitter, burnt taste of overextraction. If you have too many grounds and not enough water, the water will be spread out and you will only be able to extract the first, sour flavors of the coffee. However, on the reverse side, if you do not have enough grounds and too much water, the grounds will be overused and will produce bitter, overextracted flavors in your coffee. It is important to get a scale (or another measuring device) so you can measure exactly how much coffee and water you are using.

The standard rule of thumb for a typical drip pot is a 1:16 ratio for brewing; that is, 1 gram of coffee to 16 grams of water (or 1 ounce of coffee to 16 ounces of water, to simplify). The following chart is a basic guide for the precise ratios to use depending on your brewing method. It is important to note that the ratio should change depending on taste preference and brewing method. Try different ratios to see what you prefer yourself. This is simply a great place to start.

Quick conversions for looking at these guidelines:

1 OUNCE = about 28 grams

1 TABLESPOON = about 14 grams or ½ ounce

DEVICE	GRAMS OF COFFEE TO GRAMS OF WATER	(TYPICAL) AMOUNT OF COFFEE AND WATER USED *PER CUP*
AEROPRESS	1:12	Roughly, 17 grams coffee to 204 grams water
CLASSIC DRIP POT	1:16	Roughly, 17 grams coffee to 272 grams water
CLEVER COFFEE DRIPPER	1:16	Roughly, 17 grams coffee to 272 grams water
FRENCH PRESS	1:15	Roughly, 17 grams coffee to 255 grams water
MOKA POT	1:7	Roughly, 17 grams coffee to 119 grams water
POUR OVER	1:14 to 1:16	Roughly, 17 grams coffee to 238 to 272 grams water
SIPHON	1:15	Roughly, 17 grams coffee to 255 grams water

Rule 5: REMOVE IMPURITIES

When brewing coffee, be aware of ways you might be imparting flavors into the coffee that were not originally present. Here are a few things (among many) to keep in mind:

WET YOUR FILTER: Always wet your filter before you brew coffee in it, so it does not impart a papery taste into your drink.

PICK YOUR MUG WISELY: Plastic and many forms of metal mugs can impart flavors into your coffee. Opt for a ceramic or glass mug, as they impart the least amount of unwanted taste.

DON'T USE PLASTIC BREWERS: As with mugs, plastic brewers or tools used in brewing can impart a plastic, chemical taste into your drink via the hot water running through the device. Obviously, this is difficult to avoid due to how often plastic is used, so opt for high-quality plastic if it must be used.

BE MINDFUL OF COFFEE STORAGE: Be mindful of the container in which you store your beans or grounds, as many storage containers can impart flavors into your coffee. Avoid plastic bags and metal tins, as they add a plastic or metal taste to your drink. The best kind of storage bin is a ceramic or glazed clay pot; glass containers are also good.

Coffee Break! WATER QUALITY MATTERS

As a cup of coffee is 98 percent water, it is extremely important to use the highest-quality water possible when brewing. If you don't have pure or filtered water, the water used will impart tastes into your drink that could ruin it. Coffee shops often have very high-quality water filtration systems that cost anywhere from hundreds to thousands of dollars. For your home brewing needs, it is not necessary to buy such expensive equipment. A simple water filter pitcher or spout will dramatically reduce the contaminants within your water and will work just fine. Another option for many people is a mineral packet, which you pour into the water before you brew coffee with it to balance the minerals and pH, among other things, within the water for optimal coffee brewing.

THE BENEFITS

By using these rules, tips, and techniques, you can certainly make as good coffee as your local coffee shop—if not better. Being able to have great coffee at home can save you a tremendous amount of time and money. As the average American spends roughly $1,100 a year on coffee, making it at home is a much more economical option.

Another critical aspect to making coffee at home is the impact it has on our environment. Each coffee drinker creates about 23 pounds of waste a year through the cups, lids, straws, and sleeves that are used and discarded when buying coffee one cup at a time from a shop. By making coffee at home, you can seriously reduce the "to-go" waste that plagues our world.

The final benefit, which is what draws many people to home coffee brewing, is the full control it gives you over your cup of coffee. You can take part in the art of coffee brewing and craft amazing drinks, which can be extremely rewarding.

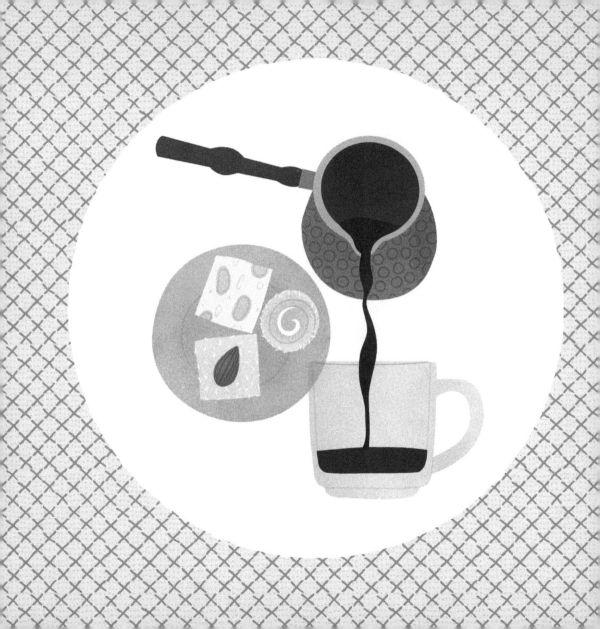

CHAPTER THREE

Coffee-Based Drinks

YOU HAVE ALREADY LEARNED THE BASICS OF MAKING A great cup of coffee. There are so many more details I would love to cover; however, if I did, you wouldn't be able to lift this book. That said, if you are longing for more information on specific brewing devices and their individual techniques, I encourage you to seek out online tutorials and see what baristas and coffee enthusiasts are doing. We include some of our favorite tutorials in the Resources section (see page 164).

Once you perfect your coffee brewing, it is time to take what you have learned and create some exciting drinks using that amazing cup of coffee. This chapter explores simple yet exciting coffee-based drinks you can make at home. All these recipes require simple ingredients you may already have in your kitchen. The recipes in this section can all be made using whatever coffee brewing device you prefer unless a particular device is noted. While these recipes have been carefully crafted in terms of ratios of ingredients, remember: You are the artist! You can change ratios, swap ingredients, and alter processes based on your personal preference. I hope these recipes will be a launchpad to inspire you to develop your own recipes to enjoy and share with others!

BEST MUGS AND GLASSWARE

Each coffee or espresso drink can certainly be served in any mug or cup of choice. However, we offer some recommendations throughout the rest of the book. Here is an overview of the different glass types that can be used for these drinks:

TINY DEMITASSE ESPRESSO MUG: Small ceramic mug that holds up to 4-ounce hot drinks.

MEDIUM CERAMIC MUG: Perfect for 6- to 10-ounce hot drinks.

LARGE CERAMIC MUG: Perfect for 10- to 14-ounce hot drinks.

TINY DEMITASSE ESPRESSO MUG

MEDIUM CERAMIC MUG

LARGE CERAMIC MUG

MEDIUM RIDGED GLASS

LARGE CLEAR GLASS

IRISH COFFEE MUG

MARTINI GLASS

ROCKS GLASS

CLEAR GLASS MUG

MEDIUM RIDGED GLASS: A clear glass with ridges on the sides that is perfect for smaller 6- to 10-ounce hot drinks containing cream. This glass doesn't have a handle and so can get very hot, which is why it is recommended for drinks with cream that may be at a slightly cooler temperature.

LARGE CLEAR GLASS: This type of glass holds 16 to 20 ounces and is great for frozen and iced coffee drinks. It also can be used for a few cocktails. It needs to be clear so you can see your beautiful creation!

IRISH COFFEE MUG: A unique, tall glass mug with a handle and a tiny stem base; it is representative of the Irish tradition and is best used for Irish-inspired drinks.

MARTINI GLASS: The iconic V-shaped glass should be used for one thing: the martini.

ROCKS GLASS: The classic, clear, straight-sided glass with a flat bottom is perfect for numerous cocktails.

CLEAR GLASS MUG: This clear mug typically holds up to 12-ounce drinks and has a handle, as it is often used for hot drinks.

**TOOLS
NEEDED**

—

**Coffee
brewing
device of
choice
(French
press recom-
mended)**

Café au Lait

Café au lait is French for "coffee with milk." As suggested by the name, this drink is straight-forward and, therefore, a great place to start to create your own drinks at home. Traditionally, café au lait consists of equal parts brewed coffee and steamed milk. To get the most tradi-tional café au lait possible, use a dark-roast bean and a French press for brewing the coffee. This is a popular breakfast beverage, typically served in a wide-rimmed bowl, although a large mug will work just fine. If you want to be just like the French, enjoy this delicious beverage with a toasted croissant.

6 ounces milk (whole milk works best)

6 ounces freshly brewed dark roast coffee

1. Place the milk in a microwave-safe container and heat on high power for about 30 seconds until it is very hot but not boiling. Alternatively, heat the milk in a small saucepan over medium heat for about 5 minutes until very hot but not boiling, watching it carefully. Do not boil the milk!

2. Combine the coffee and steamed milk in a large mug.

RECIPE TIP: The American version of this drink includes coffee made with chicory root and is said to have been made popular in Louisiana during the Civil War due to the scarcity of real coffee beans. Try chicory coffee for a New Orleans–style café au lait. You can also add some sugar to your recipe to sweeten it a bit.

SERVES

OR

TOOLS
NEEDED
—

Pitcher

—

**Filter (some
make it in a
French press
so they can
plunge it
using the
press)**

Cold Brew

Cold brew coffee can create some confusion among inexperienced coffee drinkers. The name "cold brew" refers to the actual brewing process, rather than the temperature of the drink. Although cold brew is fairly new to the American coffee scene, it is far from new in origin. There is some debate over who was the first to craft cold brew coffee, but we know it has been in existence for at least four centuries! Cold brew is significant because it uses cold or room-temperature water, rather than hot water, to extract flavors from the grounds. Cold brew is one of the simplest coffee drinks to create and is extremely versatile to use. Keep in mind, however, that cold brew requires 12-plus hours to make, as it takes much longer for cold water to extract the full flavor from the grounds.

¼ cup fresh medium-fine ground coffee, any roast

9 ounces room-temperature water

Ice, for serving

1. Place the coffee grounds in a large pitcher and add the water. Stir to combine. Refrigerate for roughly 12 hours (more or less time based on your desired strength of the brew).

2. Pour the mixture through a filter and serve it over ice! If it is too strong, add more water.

RECIPE TIP: Using a larger pitcher, you can double or triple the recipe easily to have more cold brew later. For a fun experiment, make a batch of cold brew and a batch of traditional hot coffee using the same type of grounds. Test your palate. Can you taste the difference between each one?

FUN FACT: Iced coffee and cold brew: Is there a difference? Iced coffee is simply coffee brewed hot, *then* poured over ice. Cold brew, however, is brewed using cold or room-temperature water, which requires up to 12 hours to extract all the flavor. The result is a less bitter, less acidic, but highly concentrated coffee with even more caffeine.

TOOLS
NEEDED
—

**Small pot
or saucepan
with lid**

—

**Fine-mesh
strainer or
cheesecloth**

Café de Olla (Mexican Coffee)

The café de olla, a traditional Mexican coffee beverage, gets its name from the clay pot (*olla* is Spanish for "pot") used to brew the drink. The earthy materials that make up the pot are said to give this popular Mexican beverage its particular taste. This drink is often served in small mugs made from the same clay as the pot it brews in. What makes this drink significant is that the coffee is brewed right alongside cinnamon sticks and piloncillo, an unrefined cane sugar popular in Mexico. This drink is steeped in Mexican tradition but quickly growing in popularity in the United States.

8 ounces water

½ cinnamon stick

2 tablespoons piloncillo or dark brown sugar

1 tablespoon fresh medium-coarse ground coffee (a dark Mexican roast works best for traditional flavor)

1. In a small saucepan, bring the water to a boil over high heat. Add the cinnamon stick and piloncillo. Cook, stirring until the piloncillo dissolves.

2. Add the coffee grounds and stir. Remove the pan from the heat, cover it, and let steep for 5 to 10 minutes, depending on how strong you like your brew.

3. Using a fine-mesh strainer, strain the coffee into a mug.

RECIPE TIP: To make this drink even more flavorful, add ½ clove of star anise to the water with the cinnamon and sugar.

TOOLS
NEEDED
—

Blender

Bulletproof Coffee

Bulletproof coffee is one of the newest coffee crazes out there. The concoction of mold-free coffee, grass-fed butter, and MCT (medium-chain triglyceride) oil was created by Dave Asprey, a lifestyle and health guru. Asprey came up with the idea after hiking in Tibet and drinking yak butter tea, a common beverage in Tibetan culture. Some believe that drinking bulletproof coffee can curb hunger, clear mental fog, and help promote weight loss. Although there are divided opinions about the health benefits of bulletproof coffee, the drink has rapidly grown in popularity since Asprey first posted the recipe in 2009.

8 ounces freshly brewed hot coffee

2 tablespoons unsalted grass-fed butter

½ ounce MCT oil

In a blender, combine the coffee, butter, and MCT oil. Blend until smooth.

RECIPE TIP: To acquire the supposed health benefits of this drink, it is specifically recommended to use grass-fed butter. Similarly, MCT oil, which is easily found in your local grocery store, is recommended for the original recipe; however, many people substitute coconut oil for the MCT oil.

**TOOLS
NEEDED**

—

**Traditional
Turkish cezve
or small
saucepan**

Turkish Coffee

Turkish coffee dates back to as early as the 16th century. After being introduced to the sultan, the foreign beverage quickly became a staple in Turkish culture. It wasn't long after that there were people whose sole job was to prepare coffee, and "coffeehouses" were opened for the general public. Turkish coffee is unique in its preparation and characteristics. It is prepared using a traditional Turkish coffeepot called a *cezve* or *ibrik*, which you can easily find online or in some kitchen stores. Extremely fine coffee grounds are heated directly in water until a layer of foam appears on top. The coffee is served with the grounds at the bottom of the cup, which means you consume only about two-thirds of what is served. Traditionally, Turkish coffee is served with a glass of water and something sweet to eat to counter the extreme bitterness of the drink.

**8 ounces
cold water**

**2 teaspoons
extra-finely
ground coffee**

1. In the cezve, combine the cold water and coffee. Stir gently to mix.

2. Place the pot over low heat and cook for 3 to 4 minutes, stirring occasionally, until foam starts to rise to the top. Remove the pot from the heat just before it begins to boil.

3. Using a small spoon, scoop the foam off the top of the cezve and into a small cup.

4. Return the cezve to the heat and reheat just until the coffee boils. Carefully pour the coffee into the cup. Let sit for 1 to 2 minutes until the grounds settle to the bottom.

RECIPE TIP: If you prefer your Turkish coffee sweet, add some sugar to the coffee and water before heating it. Sugar is never added to Turkish coffee after it is prepared. In addition, Turkish coffee is never served with milk. Enjoy this cup black!

TOOLS
NEEDED
—

**Vietnamese
phin coffee
filter or
French press**

Vietnamese Coffee

Coffee in Vietnam is more about ritual than caffeine consumption. The practice of making coffee is given time and thought rather than being rushed. This traditional Vietnamese coffee drink is also smaller in comparison to some, as the Vietnamese are concerned more with quality over quantity. Vietnamese coffee is known to be quite strong and bitter, so a little is really all you need. This is also why traditional Vietnamese coffee is served with sweetened condensed milk. The sweetness of the milk cuts the bitterness of the coffee, leaving you with a delicious creamy treat. A Vietnamese filter called a *phin* is recommended for this recipe; however, a French press could be used as well.

RECIPE TIP: This coffee can very easily be made into an iced coffee! Simply follow the recipe and then pour the completed beverage into a glass filled with ice!

3 tablespoons ground coffee (Vietnamese coffee or a French roast works best)

8 ounces water

½ to 1½ ounces sweetened condensed milk

1. Pour the coffee grounds into the basket of the phin and carefully put the filter on top. Place the device on top of a medium ceramic mug.

2. In a small saucepan over high heat, heat the water until just before it boils. Pour about 1 ounce (2 tablespoons) of the hot water over the filter and let the coffee "bloom" for a few seconds.

3. Continue pouring the remaining hot water into the filter. Wait for all the coffee to drip into the mug.

4. Stir in the condensed milk, as much or as little as you like, depending on how sweet you like your coffee.

PREPARATION TIP: To bloom coffee means to cover the grounds with hot water, which causes them to release their CO_2 and make it look as if the coffee is bubbling. The water takes the place of the released CO_2, and the brewing process begins.

**TOOLS
NEEDED**

—

**Small
saucepan**

—

**French press
or strainer**

Scandinavian Coffee

Scandinavian coffee originated in, you guessed it, Scandinavia (Sweden and Norway, in particular). However, it is now often attributed to parts of the American Midwest, where it likely migrated with Scandinavian immigrants. Scandinavian coffee has one consistent ingredient that cannot be replaced or substituted: a raw egg. Yes, you read that correctly. This recipe includes mixing a raw egg (including the eggshell) into your coffee grounds before boiling everything together in a pot and straining it out to leave behind a smooth, balanced cup of coffee with very little bitterness. The idea behind the egg is that because it is a natural "clarifier," it attracts the impurities in the grounds to itself rather than allowing them to pass through into your beverage. It's weird, yes, but it's also pretty darn cool.

8 ounces room-temperature water

1 large egg, carefully washed

1 tablespoon freshly ground coffee

8 ounces ice-cold water

1. In a small saucepan over high heat, bring the water to a boil.

2. Crack the egg into a glass, add the shell, and break it up in the glass.

3. Stir the coffee grounds into the egg. Add the mixture to the boiling water. Turn the heat to medium-high and boil for 5 minutes. Be careful not to let the mixture boil over!

4. Remove the pan from the heat and add the ice-cold water.

5. Carefully pour the coffee into the French press, doing your best to leave behind the egg and grounds mixture. Strain the beverage through the press to separate any stray grounds from the drink. Pour the coffee into your mug and marvel at your egg coffee.

TOOLS
NEEDED
—

Coffee brewing device

—

Small saucepan

—

Tea strainer or fine-mesh sieve

Yuanyang (Hong Kong Coffee)

Two of the most popular drinks in the world are coffee and tea, so brilliantly, someone in Hong Kong thought to combine them. Since that first revelation, this drink has been served in countless cafés and restaurants throughout China and has slowly spread its reach across the world. Tea drinkers marvel at the extra body the coffee provides, and coffee drinkers enjoy the depth the black tea adds. Next time you need to decide between coffee and tea . . . just do both!

4 ounces water

1 tablespoon black tea leaves

2 ounces half-and-half

2 tablespoons sugar

6 ounces brewed coffee

1. In a small saucepan over high heat, bring the water to a boil. Add the tea leaves, reduce the heat to low, and simmer for 3 minutes. Using a tea strainer, strain the tea into a mug. Discard the tea leaves.

2. Stir in the half-and-half, sugar, and coffee.

Cream Soda Cold Brew

Two very different drinks are combined to make this delicious summer beverage. The fizz from the soda mixed with the rich, full-bodied espresso equals a well-rounded finish. It has only been in recent years that coffee and soda have started crossing paths. There are many recipes using other types of sodas; however, cream soda is a great trial option as its flavors mimic some typical syrups used in coffee drinks. So, next time you're craving coffee on a hot summer's day, whip up this ice-cold concoction and let your cares melt away.

Ice, for serving

6 ounces cold brew (page 46)

6 ounces cream soda

1. Fill a tall glass with ice and pour in the cold brew.

2. Holding the glass at a slant, pour the cream soda into the cold brew, trying not to create too much fizz. Smile and enjoy the ride.

RECIPE TIP: To keep any cold coffee drink from becoming diluted, fill ice cube trays with cold brew and freeze them. Use these cold brew cubes in your drink—as they melt, they won't dilute your coffee!

Milk 'n' Honey Cold Brew

Coffee drinkers have been using honey as a natural sweetener for hundreds of years. While many sweeteners and syrups often overtake a drink, honey is much subtler and, instead, works as a complement, without overpowering the coffee flavors. This great mix of honey with cinnamon and vanilla really transforms some of the bitter taste of cold brew to something reminiscent of cuddling with a bunny (if that is a good thought for you).

**Ice cubes,
for serving**

**4 ounces cold brew
(page 46) or
espresso (page 66),
chilled**

4 ounces milk

1 tablespoon honey

**¼ teaspoon
vanilla extract**

**¼ teaspoon ground
cinnamon**

1. Fill a tall glass about halfway with ice and pour the cold brew over the ice.

2. Stir in the milk, honey, and vanilla.

3. Sprinkle the top with cinnamon.

RECIPE TIP: For a fall variation, add some nutmeg and brown sugar on top with the cinnamon!

CHAPTER FOUR

Classic Espresso Drinks

THIS CHAPTER INCLUDES RECIPES FOR MOST OF THE CLASSIC espresso-based drinks you might find at your favorite café. Many of these drinks have been served around the world for hundreds of years and, having stood the test of time, are now "classics." But every café puts its own spin on these drinks—and you have that same creative freedom. Adjust the ratios until you find one that fits your style and taste preferences best.

GENERAL NOTE ON MAKING ESPRESSO

Espresso is going to be the foundation for all the drinks in this chapter and many of the drinks in the following chapters. You must know how to make a great shot of espresso before you can effectively make these drinks.

As a general rule, stick to roughly 17 grams of coffee to 55 grams of water when making espresso.

I recommend using either an espresso maker, AeroPress, or Moka pot; if you do not have any of these devices, a French press would be the next best thing to use. Without any of these brewing devices, it will be challenging for you to make espresso. However, it is sometimes possible to simply add a much higher ratio of coffee grounds to water to, hopefully, produce a stronger shot of coffee similar to espresso.

Making espresso is an art that baristas spend years developing. Enjoy the process and, most importantly, enjoy the espresso!

Coffee Break! THE FOUR MAJOR COFFEE FLAVOR ELEMENTS

1 **ACIDITY:** One of the most important elements in coffee is the amount of perceived acidity. Many lighter-roast coffees and those with fruit or citrus notes often have high acidity. The easiest way to explain acidity is that it gives you the kind of "smiling feeling" in your lower jaw, like eating a lemon.

2 **BITTERNESS:** Many darker-roast coffees or grounds that have been overextracted have a lot of bitterness. If a coffee is bitter, it is often felt on the back of the roof of your mouth.

3 **MOUTHFEEL:** Mouthfeel seems very complicated to the new coffee drinker, but the word really explains itself. Does the coffee feel thick and creamy like milk or does it feel thin like tea? Is it oily or does it have a drier, astringent taste similar to red wine or green tea? These are all simple questions you can ask yourself to help you understand the mouthfeel of a particular coffee.

4 **SWEETNESS:** Green coffee beans contain natural sugar, but much of it is destroyed during the roasting process. If you're new to drinking coffee, this can be hard to discern, but many coffees have sweet notes of strawberries, blueberries, or other ripe fruits that can be distinguished from the more bitter flavors in the coffee.

TOOLS
NEEDED
—

**Espresso
brewing
device**

—

**Milk frother
or a whisk
and a glass**

Cappuccino

Cappuccino means "little cap," which is named for the Capuchin order of monks who wore their iconic brown cloaks and had shaved heads. When a cappuccino is poured well, the outer dark brown crema layer surrounding the inner circle of white foam closely resembles the head of one of these monks. The cappuccino, a classic coffee shop drink, is often confused with a latte. The difference between the two is that a cappuccino is only 6 ounces and has equal parts milk foam and steamed milk, while a latte has more steamed milk than foam and is traditionally 8 ounces.

RECIPE TIP: Cappuccinos are mostly foam when first made. However, the drink will quickly separate into equal parts steamed milk and foam after pouring, which makes for a traditional cappuccino. Try sprinkling some cocoa powder on top for a great twist to this classic drink!

**2 ounces espresso
(page 66)**

**4 ounces milk
(whole milk
works best)**

1. Pour the espresso into a mug.

2. Place the milk in a wide glass or glass jar and microwave on high power for 30 seconds until it is very hot but not boiling. Alternatively, heat the milk in a saucepan over medium heat for about 5 minutes until very hot but not boiling, watching it carefully.

3. Using a milk frother, froth the milk until you don't see any bubbles and you have a very thick froth, 20 to 30 seconds. Swirl the glass and lightly tap it on the counter repeatedly to pop the larger bubbles. Repeat this step as needed.

4. Using a spoon to hold back the foam (it should be mostly foam), pour the milk into the espresso. Spoon the remaining foam on top.

TOOLS NEEDED

—

Espresso brewing device

—

Milk frother or a whisk and a glass

Café Latte

A café latte is an espresso-based drink consisting of one-third espresso and two-thirds steamed milk with a small amount of foam to top it off. The term *café latte* is Italian for "coffee and milk." Most of the time, a "coffee" in Italy means espresso, which explains why this drink is made of espresso and milk rather than coffee and milk. The café latte has become one of the most popular espresso drinks around and is known in the United States as simply a "latte." However, be fore-warned: When ordering a "latte" in Italy, you might end up with a glass of warm milk!

RECIPE TIP: There are lots of ways to experiment with café latte. For a dairy-free version, replace the whole milk with a milk alternative, such as soy, oat, or coconut milk. You can also experiment by adding flavor to your lattes, such as caramel, vanilla, or blackberry syrup.

**2 ounces espresso
(page 66)**

**10 ounces milk
(whole milk
works best)**

1. Pour the espresso into a mug.

2. Place the milk in a wide glass or glass jar and microwave for about 30 seconds until it is very hot but not boiling. Alternatively, heat the milk in a saucepan over medium heat for about 5 minutes until very hot but not boiling, watching it carefully.

3. Using a milk frother, froth the milk until you don't see any bubbles and you have a very thick froth, 20 to 30 seconds. Swirl the glass and lightly tap it on the counter repeatedly to pop the larger bubbles. Repeat this step as needed.

4. Using a spoon to hold back the foam, pour the milk into the espresso. Spoon the remaining foam on top.

FUN FACT: You can easily make this drink iced. It's actually easier than making a hot latte. Simply make the espresso and add cold milk and ice. No need for steamed milk!

**TOOLS
NEEDED**

—

**Espresso
brewing
device**

—

**Milk frother
or a whisk
and a glass**

Flat White

It is unclear whether the term "flat white" was coined in Australia or New Zealand, but we do know the drink is basically a cappuccino without the foam. The flat white became popular in the United States after Starbucks added it to their menu. The flat white is very similar to a cappuccino but has no foam at all. You might order a flat white when you want an espresso drink that is a bit stronger than a latte but without as much foam as a cappuccino.

2 ounces espresso (page 66)

4 ounces milk (whole milk works best)

RECIPE TIP:

If you are attempting to make a flat white the way Starbucks does, use 12 ounces of milk instead of 4 ounces and only 1 ounce of espresso.

1. Pour the espresso into a mug.

2. Place the milk in a wide glass or glass jar and microwave for 30 seconds until it is very hot but not boiling. Alternatively, heat the milk in a saucepan over medium heat for about 5 minutes until very hot but not boiling, watching it carefully.

3. Using a milk frother, froth the milk until you don't see any bubbles and you have a very thick froth, 20 to 30 seconds. Swirl the glass and lightly tap it on the counter repeatedly to pop the larger bubbles. Repeat this step as needed.

4. Scoop out and discard any foam on top of the steamed milk. Pour the milk into the center of the espresso, making a tiny white circle in the middle.

SERVES

1

TOOLS
NEEDED

—

**Espresso
brewing
device**

—

**Milk frother
or a whisk
and a glass**

Macchiato

Depending on where you were first introduced to this drink, you might be a bit alarmed at our recipe. Popular chain coffee shops have, for some reason, re-coined the term "macchiato" to mean an unmixed latte with the espresso on top and the milk on the bottom, typically served iced. This is by no means a traditional macchiato, and no one is quite sure why the two drinks share the same name. The traditional macchiato is simply espresso cut with a little cream. This drink is perfect for someone who enjoys the flavor of espresso but just needs it to be cut a little with some milk without diluting it too much.

2 ounces espresso (page 66)

1 ounce milk (whole milk works best)

1. Pour the espresso into a mug.

2. Place the milk in a wide glass or glass jar and microwave for 30 seconds until it is very hot but not boiling. Alternatively, heat the milk in a saucepan over medium heat for about 5 minutes until very hot but not boiling, watching it carefully.

3. Using a milk frother, froth the milk until you don't see any bubbles and you have a very thick froth, 20 to 30 seconds. Swirl the glass and lightly tap it on the counter repeatedly to pop the larger bubbles. Repeat this step as needed.

4. Scoop out a dollop of foam and put it on top of your espresso.

RECIPE TIP: If you were hoping for the other kind of macchiato, pour 10 ounces of milk over ice and add 2 ounces of espresso over the top, unmixed. If you go this route, you might as well add some caramel sauce (see ingredient tip, page 92) to top it off!

SERVES

1

TOOLS
NEEDED
—

**Espresso
brewing
device**

Americano

The tale is often told that the Americano got its name from a bunch of wimpy Americans who couldn't handle full-strength espresso. The story goes that during World War II when American GIs were stationed in Italy and ordered espresso, they would often water it down so they could handle the bitterness. It has not been proven whether this is accurate, but most coffee professionals tend to believe it's true. The Americano we have today is the same as it has always been: espresso diluted with hot water. The beauty of the Americano is that it allows you to drink espresso and it lasts much longer than the classic 2-ounce drink. When you want something more full-bodied than a classic cup of coffee, the Americano is a surefire pick.

**2 ounces espresso
(page 66)**

**6 to 10 ounces
hot water**

**Cream, for serving
(optional)**

**Sugar, for serving
(optional)**

Pour the espresso into a mug and add hot water to dilute, depending on how strong you like your brew. Enjoy it black or add cream and sugar, as you like.

TOOLS
NEEDED

—

**Espresso
brewing
device**

—

**Coffee
brewing
device**

Red Eye

The red eye often finds itself in the hands of a college student working on a paper around 3 a.m. (hence the name). It is what sleep-deprived people desperately lean on to keep them moving. It is simply an entire cup of coffee with a double shot of espresso added. For those who can handle the caffeine and enjoy a strong cup of coffee, this is an ideal drink. With the right espresso and coffee combination, this can be an amazingly rich, full-bodied drink that will surely awaken the senses.

**2 ounces espresso
(page 66)**

**10 ounces
brewed coffee**

**Cream, for serving
(optional)**

**Sugar, for serving
(optional)**

In a mug, combine the espresso and coffee.
Enjoy it black or add cream and sugar
to taste.

RECIPE TIP: If you can brew both the espresso and coffee at the
same time, that is ideal, so one does not cool. However, if you
have to do one at a time, make the espresso first, then the
coffee so your drink stays warm longer.

SERVES

TOOLS
NEEDED
—

**Espresso
brewing
device**

—

**Milk frother
or a whisk
and a glass**

Cortado

The cortado is common in many Latin American countries, and although it can be found in North American cafés, it is less commonly ordered. The word *cortado* means "cut" in Spanish. The drink was given this name because it consists of a shot of espresso "cut" with equal parts warm milk. What sets this drink apart from other drinks made with espresso and milk is that the milk is typically not texturized. Italians tend to texturize their milk, resulting in more foam on top, whereas Spanish coffee drinks are made with steamed milk that is not texturized, so you won't see as many bubbles in your frothed milk.

**2 ounces espresso
(page 66)**

**2 ounces milk
(whole milk
works best)**

1. Pour the espresso into a mug.

2. Place the milk in a wide glass or glass jar
   and microwave for 20 to 30 seconds until
   it is very hot but not boiling, watching it
   carefully. If you have a food thermometer,
   aim for between 115°F and 125°F.

3. Using a milk frother, froth the milk only
   until you have a very light froth, about
   10 seconds. Swirl the glass and lightly tap
   it on the counter repeatedly to pop the
   larger bubbles. Repeat this step
   as needed.

4. Pour the milk into the espresso.

TOOLS
NEEDED

—

**Espresso
brewing
device**

Espresso con Panna

Espresso con panna, in Italian, literally translates to "espresso with cream," which is all it is. While the amount of whipped cream you use can vary, it essentially is just espresso with whipped cream on top! This is a delicious drink for someone who enjoys the taste of espresso but who prefers it with a bit of sweetness. The bitterness of the espresso up against the stark contrast of sweet whipped cream provides a delightful spectrum of flavors from such a simple, classic drink.

**2 ounces espresso
(page 66)**

**Whipped cream,
for topping**

Pour the espresso into a mug and add a dollop of whipped cream on top.

RECIPE TIP: Make your own whipped cream with heavy (whipping) cream by whisking or using a hand mixer until you get stiff peaks. Experiment with adding flavor to your whipped cream to make your own version of this drink. Homemade maple-brown sugar whipped cream is delicious!

SERVES

TOOLS
NEEDED
—

**Espresso
brewing
device**

—

**Milk frother
or a whisk
and a glass**

Breve

The breve is ultimately just a latte made with half-and-half instead of milk. This simple change results in a stark contrast between the two drinks. A breve has a much creamier mouthfeel when compared to the latte. Also, the nature of half-and-half makes the breve taste a little sweeter. Often, due to its sweetness, many people call the breve the "dessert latte" and have it after dinner; however, it can be enjoyed any time of day just as easily.

**2 ounces espresso
(page 66)**

**10 ounces
half-and-half**

RECIPE TIP:
You can also make this an "iced" breve by just adding cold half-and-half to your espresso! It is a delicious alternative for a hot day!

1. Pour the espresso into a mug.

2. Place the half-and-half in a wide glass or glass jar and microwave for 20 to 30 seconds until it is very hot but not boiling. Alternatively, heat the half-and-half in a saucepan over medium heat for about 5 minutes until very hot but not boiling, watching it carefully.

3. Using a milk frother, froth the half-and-half until you don't see any bubbles and you have a medium-thick froth, 20 to 30 seconds. Swirl the glass and lightly tap it on the counter repeatedly to pop the larger bubbles. Repeat this step as needed.

4. Using a spoon to hold back the foam, pour the half-and-half into the espresso. Spoon the remaining foam on top.

TOOLS
NEEDED

—

**Espresso
brewing
device**

—

**Milk frother
or a whisk
and a glass**

Cubano

The Cubano is the one drink in this chapter that is probably the least "classic." Many cafés offer a drink similar to this recipe; however, it can vary greatly from place to place. There are so many ways to make this drink—for example, with no salt, double sugar, honey, brown sugar, cayenne, etc. The only consistency to this drink is that it is basically a latte made with half-and-half instead of milk and with something added on top. Get creative: Take the bones of this recipe and run with it as you please.

**2 ounces espresso
(page 66)**

**1 teaspoon
raw sugar**

**10 ounces
half-and-half**

Pinch sea salt

RECIPE TIP:
If you're brave,
switch out the
raw sugar for
cayenne pepper
for a spicy twist!

1. Pour the espresso into a mug and add the sugar.

2. Place the half-and-half in a wide glass or glass jar and microwave for 20 to 30 seconds until it is very hot but not boiling. Alternatively, heat the milk in a saucepan over medium heat for about 5 minutes until very hot but not boiling, watching it carefully.

3. Using a milk frother, froth the half-and-half until you don't see any bubbles and you have a medium-thick froth, 20 to 30 seconds. Swirl the glass and lightly tap it on the counter repeatedly to pop the larger bubbles. Repeat this step as needed.

4. Using a spoon to hold back the foam, pour the half-and-half into the espresso. Spoon the remaining foam on top.

5. Sprinkle on a pinch of sea salt to finish.

CHAPTER FIVE

Flavored Lattes

THIS CHAPTER BUILDS ON THE FOUNDATION OF THE CLASSIC hot or iced latte and offers ideas and techniques to take it a step further and transform your drinks in some creative ways. Within the world of specialty coffee shops, the latte seems to be the most common drink to transform into a signature drink. Baristas and home coffee brewers alike work diligently to put their own spin on this classic. Every day there are hundreds of new lattes invented using almost every ingredient and combination imaginable! Within this chapter, I have some of the most common and, in my opinion, most delicious latte recipes you can easily make at home with simple ingredients. You can also make all these recipes with whatever espresso brewing and milk frothing devices you prefer.

Once you feel comfortable with these, experiment with new combinations using whatever you have in your pantry. You may just be surprised at the delicious drinks you create!

TOOLS NEEDED

—

Espresso brewing device

—

Milk frother or a whisk and a glass

Vanilla Latte

What could be more classic than a vanilla latte? Regardless of the time of year, the weather, or the mood you are in, this drink remains one of most popular choices in coffee shops. Next time you are about to spend $5 on your third vanilla latte in one week, consider using this simple recipe to make it at home! Your wallet will thank you.

**2 ounces espresso
(page 66)**

10 ounces milk

**½ teaspoon
vanilla extract**

1 teaspoon sugar

RECIPE TIP:
Omit the
sugar for an
unsweetened
vanilla latte.

1. Pour the espresso into a mug.

2. Place the milk in a wide glass or glass jar
   and microwave for 30 seconds until it is
   very hot but not boiling. Alternatively, heat
   the milk in a saucepan over medium heat
   for about 5 minutes until very hot but not
   boiling, watching it carefully.

3. Add the vanilla and sugar to the hot milk
   and stir until the sugar dissolves.

4. Using a milk frother, froth the milk until you
   don't see any bubbles and you have a thick
   froth, 20 to 30 seconds. Swirl the glass and
   lightly tap it on the counter repeatedly to
   pop the larger bubbles. Repeat this step
   as needed.

5. Using a spoon to hold back the foam,
   pour the sweetened vanilla milk into the
   espresso. Spoon the remaining foam
   on top.

**TOOLS
NEEDED**

—

**Espresso
brewing
device**

**Milk frother
or a whisk
and a glass**

—

**Saucepan
(if making
the caramel
sauce)**

Caramel Latte

Another classic in the world of lattes is the caramel latte. Almost every coffee shop has one on its menu, and for good reason. The caramel latte is as easy to make as finding caramel sauce or syrup and adding it to a latte! Many shops even make their own caramel syrup for that extra boost of flavor. For this recipe, we recommend looking for a premium caramel sauce or making your own for the highest quality and freshest taste possible!

INGREDIENT TIP: Make your own caramel sauce! It's less expensive and easy to do. In a saucepan over medium-high heat, cook 1 cup sugar, whisking constantly, for about 10 minutes until it melts. Add 6 tablespoons salted butter and whisk until melted and combined. Pour in ½ cup heavy (whipping) cream while whisking. Let cool for about 15 minutes before using.

2 ounces espresso
(page 66)

10 ounces milk

2 tablespoons
homemade
caramel sauce
(see ingredient tip
on page 92) or
store-bought
caramel sauce, plus
more for drizzling

1 tablespoon sugar
(optional)

1. Pour the espresso into a mug.

2. Place the milk in a wide glass or glass jar and microwave for 30 seconds until it is very hot but not boiling. Alternatively, heat the milk in a saucepan over medium heat for about 5 minutes until very hot but not boiling, watching it carefully.

3. Add the caramel sauce and sugar (if using) to the hot milk and stir until they dissolve.

4. Using a milk frother, froth the milk until you don't see any bubbles and you have a thick froth, 20 to 30 seconds. Swirl the glass and lightly tap it on the counter repeatedly to pop the larger bubbles. Repeat this step as needed.

5. Using a spoon to hold back the foam, pour the milk into the espresso. Spoon the remaining foam on top.

6. Drizzle the top with more caramel sauce.

CONTINUED»

Caramel Latte CONTINUED

RECIPE TIP: To make this a salted caramel latte, add a pinch of salt when stirring in the caramel and sugar and top off with an additional pinch of salt over the caramel drizzle to finish.

FUN FACT: Lattes are so popular there is even a craze within the barista world to create "latte art." If you haven't heard this term before, it refers to the leaf, flower, heart, swan, or other milk design seen atop a finished latte at a specialty coffee shop. Some baristas have taken it to the next level by using different dyes and extracts to make colorful masterpieces atop their lattes. Look around your city to see if there are any upcoming latte art competitions near you and go watch!

Coffee Break! QUICK THOUGHTS ON COFFEE AND HEALTH

GREAT FOR YOUR LIVER! Studies have shown that high levels of coffee consumption are linked to a lower level of inflammation and damage to the liver.

YOUR HEART MAY LOVE COFFEE, TOO! Studies have linked coffee drinkers with having decreased rates of heart disease and more protection against arterial damage when compared to non-coffee drinkers.

EXCELLENT SOURCE OF ANTIOXIDANTS! Coffee contains more than 1,000 anti-oxidants, which are wonderfully beneficial for your body. These antioxidants keep us healthy and protect our cells from damage.

YOUR BRAIN WILL THANK YOU! Coffee has certainly been linked to a short-term memory boost, and it has also been linked to preventing long-term cognitive decline should you stay a regular coffee drinker.

CONCLUSION: While coffee is certainly not a "medicine" in itself, there are numerous benefits to making it a part of your daily lifestyle. Keep in mind, though, we're primarily talking about black coffee—not the one loaded with cream, sugar, and various sweeteners. If you want to adjust your coffee add-ins, consider replacing sugar and milk with honey and almond milk or similar alternatives, which have also been linked to positive effects on overall health.

TOOLS
NEEDED

———

**Espresso
brewing
device**

———

**Milk frother
or whisk and
a glass**

Café Mocha

A coffee shop classic, this drink's name has a history many are unaware of. The word *mocha*, though commonly thought of as a combination of chocolate and coffee, actually refers to the Yemen town, Al-Makha, from which coffee was exported around the world as early as the mid-1700s. The type of beans coming out of Al-Makha quickly took on the name "mocha" and are said to have somewhat of a chocolate flavor. Somewhere along the way, as coffee spread around the world and it was discovered how delicious it is paired with chocolate, "mocha" became a name synonymous with this combination. However, the specific term "café mocha" as it refers to a latte with chocolate syrup or powder was most likely invented in America.

2 ounces espresso (page 66)

2 tablespoons chocolate syrup

¼ teaspoon vanilla extract

10 ounces milk

Whipped cream, for garnish

1. Pour the espresso into a mug.

2. Stir in the chocolate syrup and vanilla until combined.

3. Place the milk in a wide glass or glass jar and microwave for 20 to 30 seconds until it is very hot but not boiling. Alternatively, heat the milk in a saucepan over medium heat for about 5 minutes until very hot but not boiling, watching it carefully.

4. Using a milk frother, froth the milk until you don't see any bubbles and you have a thick froth, 20 to 30 seconds. Swirl the glass and lightly tap it on the counter repeatedly to pop the larger bubbles. Repeat this step as needed.

5. Using a spoon to hold back the foam, pour the milk into the espresso. Spoon the remaining foam on top.

6. Top with whipped cream, as desired.

CONTINUED»

Café Mocha CONTINUED

RECIPE TIP: For best results, use high-quality chocolate syrup. Even better, make your own from scratch! In a saucepan over medium heat, whisk together 1 cup unsweetened cocoa powder, 1 cup sugar, 1 cup water, and ¼ teaspoon salt until boiling. Continue boiling for another 3 to 4 minutes, then remove from heat and stir in 1 tablespoon vanilla extract and cool. It will thicken more after being chilled.

TOOLS NEEDED

Espresso brewing device

Fine-mesh sieve

Milk frother or a whisk and a glass

Lavender Latte

"Nothing beats cuddling up on the couch with a soft blanket and a good book while sipping a warm lavender latte."—My wife

This drink is relatively new to the coffee scene, but not lacking in popularity. It is difficult to say who first invented the lavender latte, but whoever it was, was brilliant. Lavender has been used for thousands of years as a calming remedy, which makes it great to pair with coffee to lessen the effects of the caffeine. The two counteract each other just enough to give you a soothing, stress-relieving drink, while still benefiting from the energy and focus often brought on by caffeine.

CONTINUED»

Lavender Latte CONTINUED

2 ounces espresso (page 66)

10 ounces milk

1 teaspoon culinary-grade lavender buds (available online and in some grocery stores)

1 teaspoon honey, plus more as needed

1. Pour the espresso into a mug.

2. In a small saucepan over medium heat, combine the milk, lavender, and honey. Heat for about 5 minutes until simmering, watching it carefully. Using a fine-mesh sieve, strain the milk into a wide glass or glass jar. Discard the lavender buds.

3. Using a milk frother, froth the milk until you don't see any bubbles and you have a thick froth, 20 to 30 seconds. Swirl the glass and lightly tap it on the counter repeatedly to pop the larger bubbles. Repeat this step as needed.

4. Using a spoon to hold back the foam, pour the milk into the espresso. Spoon the remaining foam on top.

RECIPE TIP: To make multiple lavender lattes, make a batch of lavender simple syrup to use instead of the lavender and honey mixture. In a small saucepan over high heat, combine ½ cup water and ¼ cup culinary-grade lavender buds and bring to a boil. Turn the heat to low and simmer for 2 minutes. Remove from the heat and let cool before straining out the lavender buds. Combine ½ cup white sugar with half of the lavender water and simmer for another 3 to 4 minutes, stirring occasionally. Stir in the remaining lavender water and cook, stirring, until the sugar fully dissolves. Keep refrigerated in an airtight container for up to 2 weeks and use 1 to 2 tablespoons to make each lavender latte.

**TOOLS
NEEDED**

—

**Espresso
brewing
device**

—

**Milk frother
or a whisk
and a glass**

Pumpkin Spice Latte

The quintessential fall drink. This drink originated in 2003 when Starbucks employee Peter Dukes suggested it as an addition to the new fall menu. No one had any clue what a hit this beverage would become. Today, you can find the "PSL," or something very similar to it, on almost every coffee shop menu at the first sign of changing leaves—and even before! For many people, it has become a marker of the official beginning of fall.

RECIPE TIP: The maple syrup will sweeten the drink. If you prefer a drink that is less sweet, with a more pronounced pumpkin flavor, omit it or adjust the amount you use.

2 ounces espresso (page 66)

10 ounces milk

1 tablespoon canned pumpkin purée

1 tablespoon pure maple syrup (optional)

1 teaspoon vanilla extract

½ teaspoon pumpkin pie spice

1. Pour the espresso into a mug.

2. In a small saucepan over medium heat, combine the milk, pumpkin, maple syrup (if using), vanilla, and pumpkin pie spice. Heat for about 5 minutes until very hot but not boiling, stirring continuously. Pour the hot milk mixture into a wide glass or glass jar.

3. Using a milk frother, froth the milk until you don't see any bubbles and you have a thick froth, 20 to 30 seconds. Swirl the glass and lightly tap it on the counter repeatedly to pop the larger bubbles. Repeat this step as needed.

4. Using a spoon to hold back the foam, pour the milk into the espresso. Spoon the remaining foam on top. Enjoy while watching the leaves fall from the trees.

Gingerbread Latte

This is like drinking a gingerbread cookie. As soon as winter rolls around, we all start craving those holiday flavors. What better way to enjoy them than in a nice warm beverage? Cozy up next to the fireplace and watch snowflakes fall while you drink this Christmas in a cup.

RECIPE TIP: Experiment with other winter spices, such as allspice or clove, in this drink. You can also top it off with home-made whipped cream and a little gingerbread cookie to turn this beverage into a dessert.

2 ounces espresso
(page 66)

2 teaspoons
molasses

1 teaspoon light
brown sugar, plus
more as needed

½ teaspoon ground
cinnamon

½ teaspoon
ground ginger

¼ teaspoon
vanilla extract

⅛ teaspoon
ground nutmeg

10 ounces milk

1. Pour the espresso into a mug.

2. Stir in the molasses, brown sugar, cinnamon, ginger, vanilla, and nutmeg.

3. Place the milk in a wide glass or glass jar and microwave for 30 seconds until it is very hot but not boiling. Alternatively, heat the milk in a saucepan over medium heat for about 5 minutes until very hot but not boiling, watching it carefully.

4. Using a milk frother, froth the milk until you don't see any bubbles and you have a thick froth, 20 to 30 seconds. Swirl the glass and lightly tap it on the counter repeatedly to pop the larger bubbles. Repeat this step as needed.

5. Using a spoon to hold back the foam, pour the milk into the espresso. Spoon the remaining foam on top.

TOOLS
NEEDED
—

**Espresso
brewing
device**

—

**Milk frother
or a whisk
and a glass**

Maple Latte

This drink might as well be the state coffee of Vermont. It is another extremely simple latte to make at home with ingredients you probably already have in your kitchen. And yet, the result is something so delicious you'll come back to it time and again. Maple-based beverages became a hit in the coffee world a couple of years ago and were projected to become the next pumpkin spice. While they don't seem to have replaced the pumpkin spice latte, they have definitely increased in popularity.

RECIPE TIP: To add even more flavor to this already delicious latte, add ¼ teaspoon vanilla extract and a pinch of ground cinnamon to the milk before heating it up.

2 ounces espresso (page 66)

1 to 2 tablespoons pure maple syrup

10 ounces milk

Ground cinnamon, for topping

1. Pour the espresso into a mug and stir in the maple syrup.

2. Place the milk in a wide glass or glass jar and microwave for 30 seconds until it is very hot but not boiling. Alternatively, heat the milk in a saucepan over medium heat for about 5 minutes until very hot but not boiling, watching it carefully.

3. Using a milk frother, froth the milk until you don't see any bubbles and you have a thick froth, 20 to 30 seconds. Swirl the glass and lightly tap it on the counter repeatedly to pop the larger bubbles. Repeat this step as needed.

4. Using a spoon to hold back the foam, pour the milk into the espresso. Spoon the remaining foam on top.

5. Sprinkle the latte with cinnamon.

TOOLS NEEDED

—

Espresso brewing device

—

Milk frother or a whisk and a glass

Dirty Chai Latte

Can't decide between chai tea and a latte? Choose both! Masala chai is a spiced black tea from India that made its way to the States and is now common in most coffee shops. The spices typically used in this tea are clove, cardamom, cinnamon, ginger, and black pepper. A dirty chai simply mixes masala chai with a shot of espresso and milk. This drink offers the warm, spicy flavors of the chai tea combined with the smooth, sweet flavors of a latte—not to mention a little extra caffeine.

1 chai tea bag

**4 ounces
boiling water**

**2 ounces espresso
(page 66)**

Sugar, for serving

6 ounces milk

RECIPE TIP:

You can also use
chai tea concen-
trate instead
of brewing the
chai tea bag.
Simply replace
the brewed
chai tea with
4 ounces chai
tea concentrate.

1. In a mug, combine the tea bag and boiling water. Let steep for 6 minutes. Remove and discard the tea bag.

2. Pour the espresso into the chai tea and sweeten with sugar, as desired.

3. Place the milk in a wide glass or glass jar and microwave for 30 seconds until it is very hot but not boiling. Alternatively, heat the milk in a saucepan over medium heat for about 5 minutes until very hot but not boiling, watching it carefully.

4. Using a milk frother, froth the milk until you don't see any bubbles and you have a thick froth, 20 to 30 seconds. Swirl the glass and lightly tap it on the counter repeatedly to pop the larger bubbles. Repeat this step as needed.

5. Using a spoon to hold back the foam, pour the milk into the chai-espresso mixture. Spoon the remaining foam on top.

TOOLS
NEEDED

—

**Espresso
brewing
device**

—

**Milk frother
or a whisk
and a glass**

Dirty Matcha Latte

Matcha tea is another tea lover's favorite. Traditionally made in Japan, matcha is made from specially grown green tea leaves that are very finely ground into a powder and mixed with water to create a delicious earthy-tasting beverage. Matcha is high in antioxidants, which give this drink some added health benefits. Similar to the Dirty Chai Latte (page 108), the dirty matcha latte is simply a matcha latte combined with a shot of espresso. Once again, it adds a little extra caffeine to your normal coffee routine due to the caffeine content in the green tea. If you are looking to switch up your mundane morning coffee routine, give this drink a try!

2 ounces espresso (page 66)

8 ounces milk

1 teaspoon premium unsweetened matcha powder

Sugar, to taste (optional)

1. Pour the espresso into a mug.

2. In a small saucepan over medium heat, combine the milk, matcha, and sugar (if using). Heat the mixture for about 5 minutes until it is hot but not boiling, stirring continuously.

3. Using a milk frother, froth the milk until you don't see any bubbles and you have a thick froth, 20 to 30 seconds. Swirl the glass and lightly tap it on the counter repeatedly to pop the larger bubbles. Repeat this step as needed.

4. Using a spoon to hold back the foam, pour the matcha milk into the espresso. Spoon the remaining foam on top.

RECIPE TIP: Matcha powders come in many varieties. The best-quality matcha powder is labeled "ceremonial matcha." This will also be the most expensive. If you would like to avoid the higher cost, a culinary-grade matcha powder will work just fine. Matcha is easily found online, as well as at most Asian markets.

SERVES

TOOLS
NEEDED
—

**Espresso
brewing
device**
—

**Milk frother
or a whisk
and a glass**

Cinnamon Honey Latte

This cinnamon honey latte is a great pick for a day when you want something a little different than the traditional latte flavors. This warm drink will make you feel like you're sitting at Grandma's kitchen table, waiting for her fresh snickerdoodles to come out of the oven. The warmth from the cinnamon and sweetness from the honey and vanilla offer the perfect balance for your first cup of the day or your last cup before bed (decaf, of course!).

2 ounces espresso
(page 68)

2 teaspoons honey,
plus more
for garnish

½ teaspoon
vanilla extract

¼ teaspoon ground
cinnamon, plus
more for garnish

10 ounces milk

1. Pour the espresso into a mug and stir in the honey, vanilla, and cinnamon.

2. Place the milk in a wide glass or glass jar and microwave for 30 seconds until it is very hot but not boiling. Alternatively, heat the milk in a saucepan over medium heat for about 5 minutes until very hot but not boiling, watching it carefully.

3. Using a milk frother, froth the milk until you don't see any bubbles and you have a thick froth, 20 to 30 seconds. Swirl the glass and lightly tap it on the counter repeatedly to pop the larger bubbles. Repeat this step as needed.

4. Using a spoon to hold back the foam, pour the milk into the espresso mixture. Spoon the remaining foam on top.

5. Served garnished with a sprinkle of cinnamon and a drizzle of honey.

CHAPTER SIX

Frozen Drinks & Milkshakes

FOR MANY COFFEE DRINKERS, THIS SECTION FEATURES THE drinks that first lured them into the wide world of coffee. These drinks are often the gateway for turning those who aren't used to the bitter taste of coffee into lifelong coffee drinkers. Sweetly blended with ice cream, sugar, and various flavorings, it is clear why these are often the first thing new coffee drinkers try. Not only are these commonly the "entry-level" coffee drinks, but even coffee connoisseurs come back to these drinks for dessert or a cool-down on a hot day. The downside to these drinks is how expensive they can be at coffee shops. Ranging from $4 to $7 each depending on the shop, these drinks can certainly put a hole in your wallet!

In this chapter, you will learn how to easily make these drinks at home so you can start saving money and customizing your beverages. Often, when making something at home to save money, you have to sacrifice quality—but not with these recipes. You will be able to make any frappe-style drink or coffee milkshake you typically buy in your local coffee shop and rival it.

Note, too, that most of these recipes can be made with either hot coffee, cold brew, or espresso, depending on your preference and whatever you make at home.

Coffee Break! COFFEE IS A FRUIT

Most people don't realize coffee is actually a fruit that is a little bit bigger than a blueberry. It grows on a tree and comes in different colors, such as red, orange, and yellow. What we roast, grind, and brew is just the pit from the fruit. The fruit isn't typically eaten by itself. However, there is a recent trend toward finding ways to use the coffee cherry as flour, tea, and other things.

This may seem irrelevant to the average coffee drinker. But it matters because of coffee's ability to produce many different flavors. Many coffees have a floral or citrusy, fruity flavor, whereas other coffees have a nutty or chocolaty flavor. The particular coffee cherry and where it is grown (such as elevation and terrain) affects the flavors that develop in the coffee bean.

Based on studies of the fruit, there is a recent trend called the Third Wave Coffee Movement, which is all about pulling out those fruity and hidden flavors from a coffee bean. This movement has gained a lot of traction in recent years and will probably become more prominent in coffee culture in years to come. So, next time someone asks where coffee comes from, tell them it is the pit of a fruit!

**TOOLS
NEEDED**

—

**Espresso
brewing
device**

—

Blender

Mocha Frappe

A chocolate milkshake mixed with coffee—
what could be better? On a hot summer's
afternoon working in the yard, you just need a
nice, cold, indulgent beverage afterward. Treat
yourself to this mocha frappe to hit the spot. It is
basically the blended version of a mocha latte,
but with a little vanilla ice cream added. Who
doesn't need a little more ice cream in their life?

2 ounces espresso (page 66), chilled

1 cup vanilla ice cream

1 cup ice

4 ounces milk

2 tablespoons chocolate syrup

Whipped cream, for garnish

1. In a blender, combine the espresso, ice cream, ice, milk, and chocolate syrup. Blend until smooth.

2. Serve topped with whipped cream, as desired.

RECIPE TIP: For an extra chocolaty experience, substitute chocolate ice cream for the vanilla.

Very Vanilla Frappe

Many vanilla frappes come without coffee, making them essentially vanilla milkshakes. But this recipe does not lack caffeine! Spruce up your plain old vanilla frappe with a shot of espresso to give you an energy boost and add some delicious coffee flavor. The extra boost of vanilla extract along with vanilla ice cream ensures this drink lives up to its name.

2 ounces espresso (page 66), chilled

1 cup vanilla ice cream

1 cup ice

4 ounces milk

¼ teaspoon vanilla extract

Whipped cream, for garnish

1. In a blender, combine the espresso, ice cream, ice, milk, and vanilla. Blend until smooth.

2. Serve topped with whipped cream, as desired.

FUN FACT: The Guinness world record holder for the "oldest cat" was a cat that drank coffee every morning of her life. Her name was Creme Puff, and she lived to be 38 years old!

TOOLS
NEEDED

—

**Espresso
brewing
device**

—

Blender

Mint Chocolate Chip Frappe

Another classic ice cream flavor is mint choco-late chip. Why not add coffee to it? This frozen drink has the combination of coffee and choco-late we all love with the addition of refreshing mint to seal the deal. It's sweet, smooth, and fresh.

2 ounces espresso (page 66), chilled

1 cup mint chocolate chip ice cream

1 cup ice

4 ounces milk

Chocolate chips, to taste

Whipped cream, for garnish

1. In a blender, combine the espresso, ice cream, ice, and milk. Blend until smooth.

2. Add some chocolate chips and pulse until broken up.

3. Serve topped with whipped cream, as desired.

RECIPE TIP: Add 2 tablespoons chocolate syrup for a chocolate mint–chocolate chip frappe.

TOOLS
NEEDED
—
**Espresso
brewing
device**

Blender

Salted Caramel Frappe

Salted caramel is a favorite flavor for many. The taste of salty and sweet playing tricks on your palate is somehow pleasing. The first recorded person to pair sea salt with caramel was a French chocolatier by the name of Henri Le Roux in the 1970s. Since then, the combination has taken the food world by storm, and salted caramel drinks are no exception. Let this salted caramel frappe tingle your taste buds and satisfy your sweet tooth and salty cravings all in one sip!

RECIPE TIP: For the tastiest salted caramel frappe, make your own caramel sauce (see ingredient tip, page 92).

2 ounces espresso
(page 66), chilled

1 cup vanilla
ice cream

1 cup ice

4 ounces milk

2 tablespoons
homemade
caramel sauce
(see ingredient tip,
page 92) or store-
bought caramel
sauce, plus more
for drizzling

½ teaspoon salt
(preferably fine
sea salt)

Whipped cream,
for garnish

1. In a blender, combine the espresso, ice cream, ice, milk, caramel sauce, and salt. Blend until smooth.

2. Serve topped with whipped cream, as desired, and a drizzle of caramel sauce.

**TOOLS
NEEDED**

—

**Espresso
brewing
device**

Affogato

This classic Italian dessert gets its name from the Italian word meaning "drowned." The affogato consists of a scoop of vanilla gelato "drowned" in a shot of fresh hot espresso—two quintessential Italian ingredients. This is, by far, one of the easiest coffee recipes you can find, but incredibly satisfying. Affogato would be an unexpected and sophisticated dessert to serve guests at your next dinner party. The contrasts between hot and cold, liquid and solid, and bitter and sweet make this drink a good choice for the one who can't make up their mind.

1 scoop vanilla gelato or vanilla ice cream

2 ounces espresso (page 66)

Place the gelato in a small glass, pour the espresso on top, and dig in.

RECIPE TIP: The coffee world is continuously experimenting with ways to vary this classic, and you should, too! Variations include using ice cream instead of gelato, experimenting with ice cream/gelato flavors, and adding some Irish cream or hazelnut liqueur for a spiked twist.

TOOLS NEEDED

—

Cold brew maker or coffee brewing device

—

Blender

Iced Coffee Protein Shake

We could probably all confess to, at least occasionally, skipping breakfast. But few serious coffee drinkers would dare skip their morning cup of coffee. Why not try a drink that could be breakfast *and* coffee all in one? Give your body the protein it needs to start your day well, while not giving up your routine caffeine intake. This iced coffee protein shake can be made with cold brew if you have it on hand or that leftover coffee from the previous morning you saved in the fridge just for this moment. Next time you're tempted to skip breakfast, try this yummy drink instead!

4 to 6 ounces cold brew (page 46) or chilled coffee

4 ounces milk of choice

½ ripe banana

1 scoop vanilla or chocolate protein powder

1 to 2 cups ice

1. In a blender, combine the cold brew, milk, banana, and protein powder. Blend until smooth.

2. A little at a time, add the ice and blend until the drink reaches your desired creaminess.

RECIPE TIP: Use any kind of milk you like. Our suggestion for a high-protein, dairy-free choice is unsweetened almond milk.

TOOLS
NEEDED

**Coffee
brewing
device**

Blender

Dulce de Leche Coffee Milkshake

Caramel's closest relative, dulce de leche, finds itself front and center in this recipe. If you are a dulce de leche fan, like me, you will probably need to bookmark this page. The creamy, rich, satisfying taste of dulce de leche paired with the best thing known to mankind (coffee) and the second-best thing known to mankind (ice cream) creates something that the angels probably sip on the reg.

1½ cups vanilla ice cream

6 ounces coffee, chilled

2 tablespoons dulce de leche, divided

Whipped cream, for garnish

1. In a blender, combine the ice cream, coffee, and 1 tablespoon of dulce de leche. Blend until smooth and creamy.

2. Serve topped with whipped cream, as desired, and the remaining 1 tablespoon of dulce de leche.

BONUS TIP: Have your exits clear while preparing to make this so you can make a quick getaway from those who are desperate to steal your dulce de leche coffee milkshake.

—

**Coffee
brewing
device**

—

Blender

Coconut Coffee Smoothie

Imagine being in a rush in the morning trying to make both coffee and a smoothie for breakfast. Now imagine we just combined both into one! Well stop imagining, because we did! This is a great breakfast smoothie with a little bit of a kick from the coffee that, when paired with the coconut milk and vanilla, brings out a sweet, rich flavor. Feel free to add or take away ingredients to cater to your preferences.

**4 ounces
coffee, frozen**

1 banana, frozen

**8 ounces
coconut milk**

**1 teaspoon
vanilla extract**

**Coconut flakes,
for garnish**

**Ground cinnamon,
for garnish**

1. In a blender, combine the frozen coffee, banana, coconut milk, and vanilla. Blend until smooth.

2. Serve topped with coconut or cinnamon, if you prefer a bit of extra flavor.

RECIPE TIP: Chia seeds and flaxseed are common add-ins that health-conscious folk like to throw into this recipe. If that's your thing, give it a shot!

TOOLS
NEEDED

—

**Cold brew
maker or any
coffee
brewing
device**

—

Blender

Cold Brew Milkshake

Cold brew is repeatedly praised for its smooth quality. This recipe takes the smooth factor to a new level. What could be smoother than cold brew paired with ice cream?

8 ounces cold brew (page 46), chilled

1 cup vanilla ice cream

Whipped cream, for garnish

1. In a blender, combine the cold brew and ice cream. Blend until smooth and creamy.

2. Serve topped with whipped cream, as desired.

RECIPE TIP: For a mocha cold brew, add 2 tablespoons of chocolate syrup when blending and drizzle some over the whipped cream. You can also top it with a cherry if that's your style!

TOOLS
NEEDED

—

**Espresso
brewing
device**

—

Blender

S'mores Espresso Milkshake

Campfires are never complete without making classic s'mores over the fire. What if you could bring that recipe into your kitchen and pair it with ice cream and coffee? I know it sounds too good to be true, but it is actually quite easy to do and absolutely delicious. Put the marshmallow roasting sticks to the side and head to the kitchen for this one!

2 ounces espresso
(page 66), chilled

2 cups vanilla
ice cream

¼ cup
marshmallow
creme

1 tablespoon
chocolate
syrup, divided

Whipped cream,
for garnish

1 tablespoon
crushed graham
crackers

1. In a blender, combine the espresso, ice cream, and marshmallow creme. Blend until smooth.

2. Drizzle 1½ teaspoons of chocolate syrup along the inner sides of a glass.

3. Add the milkshake to your chocolate-lined glass and top with whipped cream, as desired.

4. Drizzle the remaining 1½ teaspoons of chocolate syrup and the crushed graham crackers on top of the whipped cream.

RECIPE TIP: If you want to add a little extra to this drink, put some chocolate syrup along the rim of your glass and dip the rim into the crushed graham crackers, so you have a chocolate graham cracker rim!

CHAPTER SEVEN

Coffee Cocktails

THE COFFEE COCKTAIL IS, TO SOME PEOPLE, THE BEST OF BOTH worlds: The classic, smooth taste of coffee mixed with the punch of liqueur creates a mesmerizing experience that never disappoints. Both the craft coffee and the craft cocktail movements have seen tremendous growth in recent years. The emphasis, specifically in craft cocktails, has been on using unique ingredients that complement the various types of alcohol used.

Since the introduction of the Espresso Martini (original called the Vodka Espresso) in 1983 by Dick Bradsell, there has been a rise in cocktails mixed with coffee, cold brew, or espresso. This joining of two craft industries has resulted in an explosion of flavor possibilities as both the coffee and cocktail industries work alongside each other to perfect the ingredients and methodology used in making their drinks.

This chapter covers some of the most common drinks you can make at home. Ingredients can be easily found at your local liquor store and are paired with coffee, cold brew, or espresso. As with all other recipes in this book, adjust the level of ingredients and substitute things as needed based on necessity or preference.

P.S.: This chapter will help you make lots of friends.

Coffee Break! COFFEE AND ALCOHOL

One of the first drinks to combine coffee and alcohol was made in 1983 by a man named Dick Bradsell, who worked at the Soho Brasserie in London. A customer walked into the bar and asked Dick for a drink that would "wake her up, and [mess] her up." Naturally, the first thing that came to his mind was combining coffee and vodka! Originally, the drink—the Espresso Martini—consisted of vodka, espresso, sugar syrup, Kahlúa, and Tia Maria. However, in the years following this invention, it has taken on many different names and forms and has become a worldwide classic.

Well, his drink idea definitely woke her up and got her some liquor! But it's important to note that the age-old trick of drinking coffee to sober up does not actually work. The only real cure for alcohol overconsumption is time, which coffee, unfortunately, cannot provide! It is important to remember this as people will feel the effects of the caffeine on their energy level while under the influence and assume it has lessened the effects of the alcohol—it has not. This can get people into dangerous situations. So, keep in mind that although these drinks come with a slight energy punch, do not think for any reason that the espresso negates or mitigates the effects of the alcohol. It does not.

SERVES

TOOLS
NEEDED
—

**Coffee
brewing
device**

Irish Coffee

The origins of this age-old classic are often debated. Legend has it that it started with those little leprechauns. More reliably though, it is thought to have been created by an Irish chef named Joseph Sheridan who wanted to welcome some Americans to his restaurant with a combination of the American staple—coffee—with an Irish twist. If you are new to Irish drinks, this will surely give you a warm welcome!

8 ounces hot coffee

**2 teaspoons
brown sugar**

**1½ ounces
Irish whiskey**

**Whipped cream,
for garnish**

1. In an Irish coffee mug, stir together the coffee and brown sugar.
2. Add the whiskey and stir again.
3. Serve topped with whipped cream, as desired.

1

**Espresso
brewing
device**

**Cocktail
shaker and
strainer**

Espresso Martini

In the world of cocktails, nothing is more elegant than the classic martini. With its V-shaped glass and delicate stem, you inevitably feel 20 times cooler with one in hand. Now coffee lovers can feel cool, too, with this spin on the classic. The espresso mixed with the vodka adds a smoothness to the punch of the martini. One word of advice: Skip the olives!

2 ounces espresso
(page 66)

1 ounce vodka

1 ounce coffee
liqueur, such
as Kahlúa

Ice, for serving

3 espresso beans
(optional),
for garnish

In a cocktail shaker, combine the espresso, vodka, and coffee-flavored liqueur. Add ice, cover the shaker, and shake vigorously for 15 seconds. Strain the drink into a chilled martini glass. Garnish with espresso beans (if using).

RECIPE TIP: Some people add simple syrup to make this drink a little sweeter, but I think it tastes better a little bitter. If bitterness is not your thing, add a little simple syrup, sugar, or even some melted chocolate!

SERVES

1

TOOLS
NEEDED
—

**Espresso
brewing
device**

—

**Cocktail
shaker**

White Russian

My first experience with a White Russian was with a group of friends late at night after we were already stuffed from dinner. I was looking for something sweet to put the cherry on top of an excellent meal. The bartender suggested this drink, and I don't think there could have been a better suggestion. The coffee liqueur mixed with the heavy cream and vodka really brings this drink together for a great end to a great night. It has the vibe of dessert and coffee. You'll want to keep the ingredients stocked for this one.

Ice, for serving

2 ounces espresso (page 66)

2 ounces vodka

1 ounce coffee-flavored liqueur, such as Kahlúa

½ ounce heavy (whipping) cream

1. Fill a cocktail glass with ice.

2. In a cocktail shaker, stir together the espresso, vodka, and coffee-flavored liqueur. Pour the drink over the ice.

3. Slowly pour the heavy cream on top.

RECIPE TIP: Traditionally, this drink doesn't include espresso. However, my addiction to coffee requires me to include it here! If you want a more traditional White Russian, omit the espresso or just exchange the liqueur for espresso.

TOOLS
NEEDED

—

**Coffee
brewing
device**

Mexican Coffee

Warm ice cream? Yep! This mixture of melted vanilla ice cream, tequila, coffee-flavored liqueur, and coffee is an excellent way to sweeten an evening. The sweetness of the ice cream acts as a creamer for this hot coffee cocktail, with some tequila for a little bit of south-of-the-border flair! Add this to the menu for your next taco Tuesday!

RECIPE TIP: Experiment with other ice cream flavors but, depending on the flavor choice, be warned that you could get some strange results!

½ cup vanilla
ice cream

8 ounces coffee

½ ounce tequila

½ ounce coffee-
flavored liqueur,
such as Kahlúa

1. In a glass, melt the ice cream in the microwave.

2. Add the coffee, tequila, and coffee-flavored liqueur. Stir to combine.

FUN FACT: Have you ever fought with your spouse or partner over your morning cup of coffee? Well, if you were a wife living in Constantinople in the 16th century and your husband had not provided you with enough coffee in the morning, you would have been legally entitled to a divorce! As you can see, their marriages were built on the most important things in life!

**TOOLS
NEEDED**

—

**Espresso
brewing
device**

—

**Cocktail
shaker and
strainer**

Coffee Old-Fashioned

In the world of cocktails, the Old-Fashioned has stood the test of time. Its wide appeal lies in the fact that the drink is not so complicated that you miss any of its flavors. What better way to spice up a classic than by taking another classic (coffee) and adding it to the mix? The coffee Old-Fashioned is as simple as making a regular Old-Fashioned and adding coffee or espresso. (We think espresso is best, as it provides a more well-rounded taste.)

2 ounces espresso (page 66) or coffee

1 teaspoon light brown sugar

2 ounces bourbon

Dash chocolate bitters

Ice, for serving

1. In a cocktail shaker, combine the espresso and brown sugar, stirring until the sugar dissolves.
2. Add the bourbon and a dash of chocolate bitters and stir to combine.
3. Add ice and stir for 15 seconds.
4. Fill a rocks glass with ice and strain the drink over the ice.

RECIPE TIP: For presentation, place a lemon slice on top of the drink. It will also add a little bit of sour flavor!

TOOLS
NEEDED
—

**Coffee
brewing
device**

Bavarian Coffee

What makes this drink unique is the taste of mint from the schnapps mixed with the coffee. This beverage originated in Bavaria, Germany (hence the name), and fits itself right in with the rest of the unique Bavarian cuisine. Next time you have a big *bierwurst* loaded with sauerkraut, be sure to finish it off with this classic.

4 ounces coffee

½ ounce coffee-flavored liqueur, such as Kahlúa

½ ounce mint schnapps

1 teaspoon sugar

Whipped cream, for garnish

1. Pour the coffee into your mug and stir in the coffee-flavored liqueur, mint schnapps, and sugar.

2. Serve topped with whipped cream, as desired.

TOOLS NEEDED

—

Cold brew maker or espresso maker

—

Cocktail shaker and strainer

Bourbon Cold Brew

The rich, warm flavor combination of bourbon and cold brew coffee could not be any more perfect. This drink, popular in Kentucky, is a classic holiday dessert cocktail. Kentucky folk will argue you need to use genuine Kentucky bourbon to make it right. This isn't really necessary, but we agree it makes it a bit more special.

Ice, for chilling

4 ounces cold brew
(page 46) or
2 ounces espresso
(page 66), chilled

1 ounce bourbon

1 ounce heavy
(whipping) cream

½ ounce pure
maple syrup

Ground cinnamon,
for garnish

1. Fill a cocktail shaker with ice and add the cold brew, bourbon, heavy cream, and maple syrup. Cover and shake vigorously for 15 seconds.

2. Strain the drink into a glass and spoon whatever foam is left in the shaker onto the top of the drink, leaving the ice behind.

3. Serve sprinkled with cinnamon.

RECIPE TIP: If you do not have a cocktail shaker, use any airtight container and simply shake the ingredients inside that!

SERVES

1

TOOLS
NEEDED
—
**Coffee
brewing
device**

Café Amore Cocktail

Often dubbed a winter cocktail, the café amore will surely warm you up! The nutty, sweet flavor of this drink is very inviting on those cold evenings when you need a little extra warmth.

1 ounce cognac

1 ounce almond-flavored liqueur, such as Amaretto

8 ounces coffee

Whipped cream, for garnish

Shaved almonds, for garnish

1. In a glass, stir together the cognac and almond-flavored liqueur.

2. Add the coffee.

3. Serve topped with whipped cream and shaved almonds, as desired.

RECIPE TIP: Some crazy versions of this recipe tell you to light the cognac on fire when you put it in the glass to add a smoky flavor. If you try this, don't do it alone and be very careful!

—

Espresso machine or coffee brewing device

—

Cocktail shaker and strainer

Brazilian Iced Coffee

Brazil is known for its high-quality espresso, and that rings true in the drinks Brazilians have created using it. This recipe mixes a strong shot of espresso with cream, sugar, and coconut rum for a great South American–style drink! You may be tempted to drink five of these a day, but we recommend not doing that.

**Ice cubes,
for serving**

**4 ounces espresso
(page 66) or
strong coffee**

**2 ounces coconut
rum, such as Malibu**

**2 ounces heavy
(whipping) cream**

1 teaspoon sugar

1. Fill a glass with ice and set aside.

2. Fill a cocktail shaker with ice and add the espresso, rum, heavy cream, and sugar. Cover and shake vigorously for 15 seconds.

3. Strain the drink into the glass over the ice.

RECIPE TIP: Heavy (whipping) cream works best for this recipe, but half-and-half, milk, sweetened condensed milk, or ice cream are all fine substitutes!

TOOLS
NEEDED

—

**Coffee
brewing
device**

Nutty Irishman

This recipe will ensure you never have a boring St. Patrick's Day again! While it isn't green, it is certainly as Irish as a drink can get. This drink is most often consumed as a dessert, but it can be hard to find many bars that offer it. The delicious taste of Irish cream and whiskey paired with the naturally smooth taste of coffee is certainly a recipe for a great evening. For this drink, we recommend finding your best kilt, turning on your favorite bagpipe playlist, and doing the jig.

**1½ ounces
Irish whiskey**

1 ounce Irish cream

**1 ounce hazelnut-
flavored liqueur,
such as Frangelico**

8 ounces coffee

**Whipped cream,
for garnish**

**Ground nutmeg, for
garnish (optional)**

1. In a mug, combine the Irish whiskey, Irish cream, and hazelnut-flavored liqueur.

2. Stir in the coffee.

3. Served topped with whipped cream and sprinkled with nutmeg, as desired.

RECIPE TIP: Wet the rim of your glass with water or orange juice, which sounds strange but tastes delicious, and dip it into some finely chopped hazelnuts for a little bit of crunch!

Measurement Conversions

VOLUME EQUIVALENTS (LIQUID)

US STANDARD	US STANDARD (OUNCES)	METRIC (APPROXIMATE)
2 tablespoons	1 fl. oz.	30 mL
¼ cup	2 fl. oz.	60 mL
½ cup	4 fl. oz.	120 mL
1 cup	8 fl. oz.	240 mL
1½ cups	12 fl. oz.	355 mL
2 cups or 1 pint	16 fl. oz.	475 mL
4 cups or 1 quart	32 fl. oz.	1 L
1 gallon	128 fl. oz.	4 L

Resources

For further information on coffee culture and brewing techniques, check out these websites:

- Bluebottlecoffee.com
- Coffeemadebetter.com
- Counterculturecoffee.com
- Stumptowncoffee.com

For further reading, I recommend these books:

- *Craft Coffee: A Manual: Brewing a Better Cup at Home* by Jessica Easto (Agate Surrey, 2017)
- *The New Rules of Coffee: A Modern Guide for Everyone* by Jordan Michelman and Zachary Carlsen (Ten Speed Press, 2018)

References

Acorns. "Acorns 2017 Money Matters Report." https://sqy7rm.media
.zestyio.com/Acorns2017_MoneyMattersReport.pdf.

Guevara, Julio. "What Is 'Third Wave Coffee' and How Is It Different
to Specialty?" *Perfect Daily Grind*, April 10, 2017. https://www
.perfectdailygrind.com/2017/04/third-wave-coffee-different-specialty.

Macmillan, Amanda. "Here's Another Reason to Feel Good About
Drinking Coffee." *Time*, November 13, 2017. https://www.time
.com/5022060/coffee-health-benefits-heart.

National Coffee Association. *How to Brew Coffee: The NCA Guide to
Brewing Essentials*. https://www.ncausa.org/About-Coffee/How
-to-Brew-Coffee.

Recycling Advocates. "Single-Use Coffee Cup Reduction." Accessed
August 19, 2019. www.recyclingadvocates.org/single-use-coffee
-cup-reduction.

Wadhawan, Manav, and Ancil C. Anad. "Coffee and Liver Disease."
Journal of Clinical and Experimental Hepatology 6, no. 1
(March 2016): 40–46. doi:10.1016/j.jceh.2016.02.003.

Index

Acknowledgments

FIRST AND FOREMOST, I thank the Lord for the bean and the ability to write about it. I thank my wife for all the diapers she changed while I stared at the computer screen typing this and for the millions of times she has let me make coffee for her (the good cups and the bad cups) along the way. I thank my little baby boy, Elliot, for being so punctual at distracting me while working. Thank you, Mom and Dad, for drinking coffee in your respective manners and helping me "stunt my growth" when I was younger. Thank you to Brien, Morgan, and Samuel for obvious reasons. Thank you to Harrison, Frankie, TJ, and Trenton for introducing me to the world of better coffee when I was a wee novice. Thank you, Brandon, for allowing our dorm room to always smell like a coffee shop. Samantha, I'm sorry I made fun of you for drinking coffee. Just for name-dropping's sake, Rylee, Eli, and Erik, thank you. Thank you, Berry's, for always reminding me there is a place in the world for "non-fruity coffee." To anybody else I know, even remotely, I'm just going to go ahead and thank you. This was your doing.

About the Author

 **DANIEL LANCASTER** is the owner and roaster for Short Sleeves Coffee Co. as well as the founder of coffeemadebetter.com, a craft coffee news and culture website covering a variety of topics within the specialty coffee industry. When Daniel is not writing, roasting, brewing, or drinking coffee, he spends his time with his wife and two kids in the mountains of western North Carolina.